UNEXPECTED

BLESSINGS

AVERY

a member of Penguin Group (USA) Inc.

New York

UNEXPECTED

BLESSINGS

Finding

Hope and Healing

in the

Face of Illness

Roxanne Black

Published by the Penguin Group

Penguin Group (USA) Inc., 375 Hudson Street, New York, New York 10014, USA •
Penguin Group (Canada), 90 Eglinton Avenue East, Suite 700, Toronto, Ontario M4P 2Y3,
Canada (a division of Pearson Canada Inc.) • Penguin Books Ltd, 80 Strand,
London WC2R 0RL, England • Penguin Ireland, 25 St Stephen's Green, Dublin 2, Ireland
(a division of Penguin Books Ltd) • Penguin Group (Australia), 250 Camberwell Road,
Camberwell, Victoria 3124, Australia (a division of Pearson Australia Group Pty Ltd) •
Penguin Books India Pvt Ltd, 11 Community Centre, Panchsheel Park,
New Delhi–110 017, India • Penguin Group (NZ), 67 Apollo Drive, Rosedale, North Shore
0632, New Zealand (a division of Pearson New Zealand Ltd) • Penguin Books (South Africa)
(Pty) Ltd, 24 Sturdee Avenue, Rosebank, Johannesburg 2196, South Africa

Penguin Books Ltd, Registered Offices: 80 Strand, London WC2R 0RL, England

Most Avery books are available at special quantity discounts for bulk purchase for sales promo-
tions, premiums, fund-raising, and educational needs. Special books or book excerpts also can be
created to fit specific needs. For details, write Penguin Group (USA) Inc. Special Markets,
375 Hudson Street, New York, NY 10014.

Library of Congress Cataloging-in-Publication Data

Black, Roxanne.
Unexpected blessings : finding hope and healing in the face of illness / Roxanne Black.
p.   cm.
ISBN 978-1-58333-321-1
1. Black, Roxanne—Health.   2. Systemic lupus erythematosus—Patients—United States—
Biography.   I. Title.
RC924.5.L85B53   2008   2008025985
362.196'7720092—dc22
[B]

Printed in the United States of America
1   3   5   7   9   10   8   6   4   2

BOOK DESIGN BY AMANDA DEWEY

Neither the publisher nor the author is engaged in rendering professional advice or services to the
individual reader. The ideas, procedures, and suggestions contained in this book are not intended as
a substitute for consulting with your physician. All matters regarding your health require medical
supervision. Neither the author nor the publisher shall be liable or responsible for any loss or damage allegedly arising from any information or suggestion in this book.

While the author has made every effort to provide accurate telephone numbers and Internet ad-
dresses at the time of publication, neither the publisher nor the author assumes any responsibility for
errors, or for changes that occur after publication. Further, neither the publisher nor the author has
control over or assumes any responsibility for third-party websites or their content.

ACKNOWLEDGMENTS

This book would not have been possible without Lynn Lauber. Thank you for making this experience so wonderful. You embraced my vision with your heart and your commitment is evident in all that you have done.

To Stephanie Tade, thank you for saying yes within three minutes of our introduction, for championing the book, and for guiding me through each stage of the process.

To "Beth Grossman Makes Things Happen" (BGMTH), truer words have never been spoken. Thank you for being you.

To Megan Newman and the entire Avery team, you welcomed me into your family with open arms and I am most grateful. It has been a true joy to work with all of you. Megan, you believed in this book from day one, and I couldn't be happier that Avery is its home. Lucia Watson, your insightful edits help to enrich the content. Anne Kosmoski and Amanda Tobier, your PR and marketing suggestions are exceptional; Katya, Fred, and Paul, I greatly appreciate the special time you spent with me and the way you have championed this book. To all other members of the Penguin staff, I love being part of your team.

There are countless people who have walked with me along my path—during the rocky periods and the serene. I met each of you at exactly the right time, and I thank you for the very special gifts you brought to my life. Though I am hesitant to list names, there are several key people I must recognize:

Dr. Irving Packer and the Innovating Worthy Projects Foundation; Terrance Keenan, Marco Navarro, Joe Marx, Liisa Rand and the staff of the Robert Wood Johnson Foundation, my angels John Langan and Judith Nadell, and Mimi Herington—I will always remember all that you did to assist me.

Andrew Greene, you were the first health-care system CEO to believe in Friends' Health Connection and implement our programs into patient-care services many years ago. Thank you.

I will always be grateful to Curt Weeden, Michael Bzdak, Wendy Breiterman, Jim DeVito, and everyone at Johnson & Johnson who has stood beside me and supported my work. I am proud to recognize the amazing kindness of all Johnson & Johnson staff and the outstanding contributions your corporation makes to community organizations around the world. I applaud your credo and values, and I thank you on behalf of the countless lives you continue to touch.

To everyone involved with Friends' Health Connection, including our funders, contributors, board members, and incredible staff, thank you for all that you do. Nancy and Jane, it gives me such comfort to know I can count on you in every way. To the thousands of speakers who have shared their wisdom with our audiences, your expertise continues to improve lives.

Acknowledgments

To the many doctors, nurses, and health-care professionals who have contributed to my personal well-being, thank you. To my hero, Dr. Thomas E. Starzl, and the entire staff of the Thomas E. Starzl Transplantation Institute at the University of Pittsburgh Medical Center, it is an honor to be under your wings of care.

To all of the support staff at the countless hospitals where I have been a patient, I applaud you for the kindness and compassion you bestow, which often goes unrecognized. From the cleaning people who often prayed with me and sustained my spirit to the volunteers, chefs, and transport teams, with whom I've had many an interesting conversation, to the countless hospital rabbis, chaplains, and volunteers—you uplift me.

To Krissy, a very happy 25th. Here's to many more years to come. Tracy, I'll always remember our time together on Allgair. To my family near and far, thank you for the countless times you have rallied around me with your love.

To my college roommates, who lived with me through the failure of my kidneys, five-times-daily dialysis, the start of my organization, and the procedure of my first transplant, thank you for making some of the hardest times also some of the best. . . . Kris, Lori, and Jodi, I will always cherish all of the laughs and memories.

And finally, to all of the patients out there, those I've met in person and those whom I'm meeting through the pages of this book, you are in my heart and my prayers. I wish you countless Unexpected Blessings.

I dedicate this book to my mother, Frances Black, who gave me life and stood by my side always.

To my sister Bonnie who granted me renewed life. Thank you for bestowing upon me such an incredible gift.

To my anonymous eight-month-old kidney donor, you live on within me. I think of you each day.

To my husband, Leo, thank you for being on this journey with me and for the joy and happiness you bring to my life. I love you.

CONTENTS

AUTHOR'S NOTE

The Story of the Crane on the Cover

On August 6, 1945, when the atom bomb was dropped on Hiroshima, a young girl named Sadako Sasaki was only two years old. Sadako survived seemingly unharmed until ten years later, when she was diagnosed with leukemia, which had been dubbed "the atom bomb disease."

While in the hospital, Sadako's best friend, Chizuko, took a gold-colored piece of paper and folded a paper crane as a gift for her. He explained the ancient Japanese legend that if a person folds 1,000 paper cranes her wish will be granted.

In an attempt to achieve her dream of renewed health, Sadako folded paper cranes. As her health deteriorated, she changed her wish and dreamed of world peace, so that other children would not have to suffer from the effects of war.

Sadako folded 644 cranes but, sadly, she died before she could reach 1,000. Her classmates folded the remaining 356 and all 1,000 paper cranes were buried with her.

After Sadako's death, her classmates raised funds to erect a statue in memory of all children who died as a result of the atomic bomb. The statue symbolizes the wish for world peace and features Sadako holding a golden crane in her arms.

Each day, visitors lay paper cranes by this statue in Hiroshima to symbolize peace for children around the world. At its base lies a plaque, which reads:

"This is our cry, this is our prayer; peace in the world."

PREFACE

A favorite gift of my childhood was a model of the human body called the Visible Man. A small, anatomical model made of transparent plastic, it revealed the bones and organs and vessels of the body. I spent hours assembling him on our dining room table, removing and replacing his meaty-looking liver and tiny adenoids, tracing blood vessels that traversed his interior like a map.

My hours with the Visible Man gave me a perspective that was different from other girls my age, who were absorbed with paper dolls and comics. After working on my model, I walked around the house as if I were wearing X-ray glasses, studying my family with new appreciation. Who would have thought that tucked under my father's shirt were lungs and arteries? Who could have imagined that underneath my sisters' casual exteriors were vital organs stealthily involved in silent, miraculous business?

The Visible Man made me believe that bodies were flawless, magnificent machines, perfectly designed. In the fascinating jumble of livers and stomachs, there were never kidney stones, blockages, or tumors. So when I was diagnosed with systemic lupus at the age of fifteen, not only was I shocked, I felt betrayed.

LUPUS IS CALLED the great imitator, the disease of a thousand faces, because its symptoms vary so greatly and often mimic those of other illnesses. The word itself comes from one of the more distinctive symptoms, a butterfly rash over the cheeks and across the nose.

But when I first stood in front of the mirror, studying the red rash that had blanketed my face, I couldn't discern any pattern. None of it made sense.

I didn't realize then that the rash was only a messenger of the disorder inside me. My immune system, designed to defend and protect me against foreign intruders, had gone haywire and had begun attacking healthy cells and tissues instead.

There was a civil war going on inside of me. My body was attacking itself.

Lupus made me realize that our bodies are far more complex than the anatomy I once studied. We are also made up of subwiring and neurochemicals—a broth rich with hormones, proteins, and cellular fluids. Overlaying everything else like lacework are the exquisite variations of a person's history and environment. As singular as a snowflake, these could not be charted or fabricated in plastic. They are what make the human body such a wonderful contradiction—tough and fragile, mysterious and predictable, all at the same time.

INTRODUCTION

By all accounts I am a successful and accomplished woman. As founder of a national nonprofit organization, I have met with presidents, movie stars, and best-selling authors. But the reason I am alive today, my body stealthily involved in the silent, miraculous business of life, is because of an invisible gift that has been bestowed on me not once, but twice. As a lupus sufferer since the age of fifteen, I had kidneys so damaged that I've required two transplants—one when I was twenty-one and the other when I was thirty-five.

Tucked inside me at the moment are two tiny kidneys—my second transplant—from an eight-month-old boy whose name and identity I'll never know. In time, doctors assure me, these kidneys will mature and grow in me, as they would have grown in him, and develop into adult-size organs that will flush waste products and toxins from my body.

I don't know my kidney donor's name, where he came from, or how he died, but sometimes I try to imagine him: I see him pale-haired, dressed in a blue outfit, raised in a warm climate.

I can't allow myself to imagine the details of his death or the anguish of his parents. Yet I can still sense the compassion and love that allowed them to pass along this supreme gift to a stranger suffering from lupus-related kidney failure—tiny organs, dispatched without payment, or return receipt, into a universe of need.

A singular act of grace.

A year from now I will be allowed to write a letter of thanks that will be forwarded to these parents. This is a scene I like to visualize: my envelope being torn open, my note unfolded, my words, pressed into vellum with ballpoint, absorbed into the minds of this couple. I think of them reading in window light, perhaps with a new infant in their arms.

There's a theory in science called Bell's theorem, which claims that two particles once connected are never separated, that they are stuck together by something called space entanglement. This exists in the real world, but we can't see it. But I imagine such a connection with these phantom parents—that we are united in the web of love that is always below the surface, waiting to be perceived.

Humans come equipped with pairs of limbs and organs—eyes, legs, lungs, and ears, but only one of these sets, the kidneys, includes an organ that can be considered a spare. Perhaps due to the nature of our prehistoric diet, we possess more functioning renal tissue than is necessary for survival. Because of this, it's possible to live a full, healthy life with a single kidney.

What's impossible is living without one.

Kidneys are the only human organs that can be donated from live donors—other organs require that the donor be deceased.

I'm in the rare—and lucky—category of having been the beneficiary of both types of organ donations, from the living and the dead. In 1992, my sister Bonnie gave me her left kidney, offering it up to me with the same sisterly devotion she had always bestowed on me.

It has been suggested that the cells of living tissue may have the capacity to remember and memorize characteristics of the person to whom they once belonged. I've read studies of transplant recipients who acquire strange new abilities, characteristics, and powers similar to their donors'—a man who could suddenly speak Spanish, a woman who gained the ability to paint.

I've had no experience with this kind of cellular memory, no sudden flashes of new talent, although I briefly hoped after my sister's donation that I might acquire some of her ability to sing. What I have been left with is a profound sense of duty to pass on the lessons that I've acquired on my twenty-year journey from illness to health.

THOSE OF US who face chronic illness remember the before and after moments: the day the phone rang, or the doctor walked into your hospital room, and it was clear that life as you had known it was about to change. You discover that you have cancer or multiple sclerosis or that your child has been stricken with leukemia. You hang up the phone or walk out of the hospital feeling as if your world has been transformed. It's not simply fear that makes you so disoriented—it's because you are in the midst of experiencing a true glimpse of the great preciousness and precariousness of life.

Falling ill is like joining a private fraternity—one you would never enter voluntarily, but whose membership reveals profound truths that most of us are too busy rushing through our days to consider. In the midst of everyday life, you are suddenly jolted by your own fallibility and finiteness, by the fact that you are no more durable than the shoes on your mortal feet.

In a culture that manages to cordon off this reality as if it were the special circumstance of others, you perceive all at once that this is your fleeting, precious human life. And then it's as if a veil has been ripped from your eyes. As the poet Rilke wrote: "Just once for everything, only once."

A person doesn't have to fall ill or experience great adversity to have such realizations. But the way humans are wired, it often requires such a shock to knock off the blinders of complacency and self-absorption. It is in the face of suffering that so many of us are thrown into the depths of ourselves, and come up bearing treasures of strength, insight, and courage we never knew were there.

When I first was diagnosed with systemic lupus, I yearned for something specific—to connect with others who knew what I was experiencing. If I couldn't find them in the flesh, then I wanted to read about them, real people like me who'd struggled and survived. I didn't want romance or fiction, but true stories about transformation and courage. Before I formed my own nationwide support network, I wanted to read words that would help heal and inspire me.

But when I was young, these kinds of books were hard to find.

"If there's a book you really want to read but it hasn't been written yet, then you must write it," the writer Toni Morrison once said.

So I've set out here to write the kind of book I yearned to read myself, a book made up of separate interlocking stories or vignettes that fit together like links of a necklace.

I'll weave together the inspiration and wisdom I've received from ordinary people and celebrities alike who've taught me not just how to survive chronic illness, but also how to flourish in spite of it: Christopher and Dana Reeve and a nameless hospital cleaning lady who sang "Amazing Grace" to me; Alan Alda, Deepak Chopra, Oliver Sacks, and Naomi Judd. They've made me realize that facing the challenges of illness is really facing the challenges of life itself.

Along the way, I'll take you through my transformation from a powerless, lonely, and desperately ill teenager, through my formation of a local lupus support group that eventually blossomed into Friends' Health Connection (FHC), the national organization that I founded and ran from my hospital bed and dorm room.

I'll take you along a path zigzagged with the most unusual destinations: one day at the White House Rose garden, shaking hands with President George H. W. Bush, two days later homebound in a wheelchair; one day on Fox television, the next day back in a hospital bed.

I'll share the lessons of valor and hope, courage, and love that have been bestowed on me along the way.

My years of chronic illness have shown me that the private fraternity I thought I was entering wasn't so private at all—it was a club in which most of us would eventually become members, if not ourselves, then through friends and loved ones.

Transplants are miracles of modern medicine, and I've been doubly blessed. I vowed to my sister and the nameless eight-month-old who were my donors that my life would be worth their sacrifice. This book is part of my promise to them.

One

IN THE BEGINNING

I sat at my bedroom window in my wheelchair, watching my high school rowing team pull away from the shore, eight friends smiling and waving as they moved into the choppy water. Not long ago, I'd been one of them.

I loved everything about rowing, the feeling of freedom, the teamwork, the sense of strength and accomplishment. When I rowed, I was at peace and forgot about my problems. Not that I'd had many then. In most ways, I was a typical New Jersey teenager, a shy high school freshman who lived with her mother in a small row house that overlooked Lake's Bay. My mother and I didn't have two dimes to rub together, but with that view from our windows, we considered ourselves rich.

It was after rowing one afternoon that I had the first inkling that something might be wrong with me—a sharp stab of back pain that took my breath away.

"What's the matter?" my mother asked when she saw me wincing.

"I don't know," I said, stretching. "I guess I strained a muscle."

By evening, the pain was excruciating. My mother filled a hot bath with Epsom salts, and later gave me a heating pad. I took a couple of Tylenol and decided I'd stay away from crew practice for a few days. In my young life, this had been the antidote for any ailment. Eventually everything passed, given time and a little rest.

But not this time. Instead of decreasing, the pain grew so intense that I could barely sit up in bed the next morning.

My mother took one look at me and said, "I'm taking you to the doctor."

But by the time we arrived at the office, the pain had subsided and the doctor advised that we simply continue with the heating pad and baths.

Two days later, I developed chest pains that by evening were so acute I could barely breathe. Now I was beginning to worry.

This time the doctor prescribed antibiotics, thinking I might have an infection. The pains intensified over the next few days, then they too vanished.

This pattern of new symptoms that appeared, intensified, then vanished continued with an itchy red rash, which covered my body. After it mysteriously disappeared, my ankles swelled so severely that I was unable to fit into any of my shoes.

Although the doctor tracked my reports, took bloodwork, and examined me closely, he couldn't figure out what was wrong. My symptoms were elusive; it was hard to pin them down.

Finally he referred me to a specialist. By the day of my appointment, all my symptoms had subsided except for my swollen ankles. My mother and I arrived at his office, expecting this new doctor would prescribe another medication for what was probably an allergic reaction.

Although I'd never seen this doctor's face before, his cool, sober demeanor as we walked in gave me a sense of foreboding.

After a routine examination, he studied my bloodwork, then touched my ankles, which were so full of fluid they could be molded like lumps of clay.

Then he looked up and a strange word floated from his mouth. Lupus. I saw it, like in a cartoon caption, odd and ominous, hanging in the air.

The word meant nothing to me, but my mother's reaction did; she covered her face with her hands. In her work as a nurse, she'd spent years caring for patients with chronic illness. As I watched her sniff and take out a Kleenex, it hit me that this must be serious, something that Tylenol and bed rest weren't going to solve.

My health had always been part of my identity, something I was as certain of as my strong legs and pumping heart. Now I was being told baffling facts about kidney function, inflammation, and antibodies.

But when the doctor said I was to be admitted to a children's hospital in Philadelphia the following day for testing, I realized a chapter of my life was abruptly ending and a new one was about to start.

When I returned home, I looked up lupus in our medical dictionary: a chronic autoimmune disease, potentially debilitating and sometimes fatal, that was first discovered in the Middle Ages. The illness follows an unpredictable course, with episodes of activity, called flares, alternating with periods of remission. During a flare, the immune system attacks the body's cells and tissue, resulting in inflammation and tissue damage.

The words "sometimes fatal" stood out to me, as if they were written in blood. Just as harrowing were the lists of possible manifestations: dermatological, musculoskeletal, hematological, renal, hepatic, pulmonary. What else was there?

How had this ancient disease that only affected one in many hundreds in the United States ended up in Atlantic City, residing in a teenager like me?

For that, there was no answer.

"THERE'S ALWAYS ONE MOMENT in childhood when the door opens and lets the future in," Graham Greene wrote. I don't know if most people remember that moment, but I do.

At the children's hospital, I shared a room with a three-year-old girl with a winsome face and shiny black hair cut in a bob. She was so vibrant and lively, I assumed she was someone's daughter or sister, until I glimpsed a tiny hospital ID bracelet on her wrist.

Her name was Michelle, and we bonded from the moment we met. She brought a herd of plastic ponies to my bedside and we brushed their manes and made-up stories.

"Why's she here?" I asked when her parents arrived, looking drawn and worried.

"She has a hole in her heart," her mother told me. "She's having open-heart surgery tomorrow."

A steady stream of doctors arrived to talk to Michelle's parents. I heard the terse murmur of their voices behind the curtain that separated our room. Through it all, Michelle dashed between the beds, oblivious to the drama around her. She was so vital and energetic, it was hard to believe that anything serious was wrong with her.

I'd never known a sick child before, and now I was in a hospital full of them. It seemed unnatural seeing toddlers on IVs, babies on ventilators, adolescents with leg braces, struggling to walk. A parade of pediatric malfunction passed my door, children smashed in motor accidents, suffering from muscular dystrophy and leukemia. This alternate world had existed all along, behind my formerly sunny, innocent life.

The next day I was to find out the results of my kidney biopsy, and Michelle was headed to surgery. Before she left, she walked over and hugged me so tightly that I could smell the baby shampoo in her hair. Then she solemnly handed me a drawing she'd made of a house, a girl, and a tree.

"This is you, isn't it?"

She nodded.

"Well, it's beautiful, thanks. I'll see you later."

I waited all day for them to bring Michelle back, trying to distract myself by reading and crocheting, but it was no use. Breakfast came and went, then lunch, and still there was no sign of her.

Early in the evening, I was talking on the pay phone in the hallway when an alarm sounded, and doctors began running down the hall from all directions. A woman's voice intoned a code over the loudspeakers, a foreign babble.

As I hung up I saw two new figures running down the hallway. Their features grew terribly familiar as they approached. It was Michelle's parents, their faces smeared with tears, heading in the same direction as the doctors.

My mother came out and hurried me back into the room. When she shut the door, I stood there, looking at Michelle's bed, at the picture on the table that she had drawn for me. I took out a little prayer book I'd brought along and began a prayer, infusing it with all the love and intention I could muster. A long, terrible female scream pierced the silence.

A young floor nurse walked in a short while later. Her sad face was statement enough, but then she told us. Michelle hadn't made it. She'd suffered a heart attack and died.

So there it was, and I had to face it: Life wasn't fair. Prayers weren't always answered. The young and innocent could be lost. The door had swung open, and I had been pushed through to the other side.

THE KIDNEY BIOPSY confirmed that I indeed had systemic lupus, the most common and serious form of the disease, and that I was currently in an active stage, or flare. The doctor prescribed very high doses of steroids in an attempt to put the disease in remission. He rattled off possible side effects of these drugs— susceptibility to infection, insomnia, weight gain, depression, sensitivity to the sun.

I still couldn't believe this was happening—that my body, my old friend and companion, was betraying me this way. And what had I done wrong? I'd always been active, eaten well, and rarely even caught a cold or flu. But as in a horror movie where the werewolf watches his body alter in the mirror, mine was turning on me. The doctor's description of lupus—how the immune system actually makes a mistake and begins to attack its own tissues, corresponded with how I was feeling, as if a mutiny were taking place inside me. My own body was attacking and destroying itself.

Apart from the lupus, the steroids caused their own metamorphosis. I sat back, a bewildered observer, as my body transformed itself before my eyes. I rapidly gained weight from a new, steroid-induced appetite, and my face turned moon-shaped and swollen. My legs were striped with stretch marks from water retention and swelling; my long hair fell out in clumps.

When I passed myself in the mirror, I was stopped short by this pale, swollen creature, who would have a hard time getting into a boat, let alone rowing one.

On rare visits from old friends, I could tell that my swollen body and pill bottles made them nervous. I sat listlessly while they complained about broken nails or pimples or how much they'd spent on a pair of jeans.

I wanted to take them by the shoulders and say, "Listen!" I wanted to tell them about Michelle. But they didn't want to know about this parallel reality. And who could blame them? A few months before, I had also believed we were all golden, that our youth granted us immunity. I wasn't surprised when most of them stopped visiting.

For me, the hardest part of being sick was the isolation. With chronic illness, you enter another country, and it can feel as if you're the only inhabitant. Those you've known before are back on the other side of the mountain, in the carefree valley of the healthy, their oblivious days unmarked by blood tests or CAT scans. No matter how much they try, it's difficult for them to comprehend what you have seen from your new perspective.

I remembered overhearing older people say, "When you've got your health, you've got everything," and thinking they were crazy.

There were so many other things to want—good looks, clothes, and money. I still wanted all those things, but they had now slid far down the list of what mattered. Illness sharpens your vision and narrows your desires. You can see, all at once, just how precious life is.

ONE AFTERNOON when I hadn't been out of the house for weeks, my mother asked me to ride with her to the grocery store.

I didn't want to be out in public with my thin hair and thick ankles; I was mortified as much by how I looked as by the fact that I was ill.

"C'mon, it'll do you good," she insisted.

I relented, but laid down in the backseat so no one would see me. As I watched the telephone poles and electric wires pass by, I felt futureless. Self-pity, like a great dark bubble, burst in me. I buried my face in my hands and cried out, "Why me? Why did this have to happen to me?"

My mother studied me in the rearview mirror. "Maybe you got sick for a reason," she said after a moment. "Have you ever thought of that? Maybe you were meant to help others."

"What are you talking about? What reason? I'm the one who needs help!"

"Well, just think about it," she said.

THREE AND A HALF MONTHS LATER, when I returned to school, there were several theories about why I'd been absent so long. Since I'd left school slender and healthy and returned pale and heavy, the main rumor seemed to be that I was pregnant. As upset as I was by this gossip, I was just as concerned my classmates would discover the truth about how sick I was—or that I had a disease they might not understand.

But it was impossible to camouflage. I was too weak to climb the high school stairs anymore and instead had to take the service elevator. The kids saw me there, in my oversize Nikes, standing with the janitors between the mops and brooms. They saw me on the sidelines at gym class, watching passively while the others ran and kicked balls.

The school was the same, the world was the same, but I was different. I'd become so identified with those who were sick and suffering that I was shocked by how cavalierly my classmates treated their bodies. I'd just been with people who would have done anything to simply feel well again. Now, here were my friends, drinking and smoking, living as if their bodies were eternal, as if they could abuse and misuse them forever.

ONE EVENING WHEN A GROUP of old friends invited me out with them, I climbed into a car filled with smoke and chatter.

"He really called you? What did he say?" one girl was asking, while I shifted in the backseat, trying to find a comfortable way to arrange my painful legs.

En route to one of their houses, we stopped at the supermarket. As soon as we got out of the car and began walking toward the entrance, I realized I couldn't keep up with them. My muscles were weak, and my feet felt like two large stones. The others rushed ahead, their high heels clicking into the distance. They didn't even notice when I fell down in the middle of the busy parking lot.

I was too frail to push myself up so I sat there, knowing it was only a matter of time before a car appeared. Yet I couldn't bring myself to call out for help. It was a sobering truth—I would rather risk my life than admit my vulnerability.

Eventually I crawled over to a parked car, grabbed onto the bumper, and hoisted myself to a standing position. I gradually regained my balance and made my way inside the supermarket where I spotted my friends. I continued to trail behind them and realized they'd never even known I was missing.

In fact, the girl they thought they knew was gone for good.

Of all the many things that pained me about my illness, this was the most acute—saying good-bye to this former self, to my adept and strong body. I knew that in order to survive I'd need to find something equally compelling to which to say hello.

Was there anyone who could identify with how I was feeling, who'd been diagnosed with this disease that made me feel like a stranger in my own body? My doctor patiently answered my questions, and my mother consoled me all she could. But I yearned for something specific—another person who had literally been in my shoes—the large male Nikes, which now were the only shoes I could wear.

And if there were such people, how would I ever find them? This was before personal computers were common, let alone the Internet.

My mother's words kept echoing in my mind: maybe there was a reason.

I'd always been active in fund-raising. Whenever the Jerry Lewis

Telethon came to Atlantic City, I headed out to the boardwalk on weekends to solicit donations. In elementary school, I'd raised more money than any other kid in the school for the MS Read-a-thon. But those had been other people's diseases; now I had my own.

Even at fifteen, I realized I desperately needed companionship and connection. I made a decision: if there were no support groups in our area, I'd have to start one myself.

I had been regularly seeing a lupus specialist, Dr. DeHoratius, who was based in Philadelphia, and I asked if he'd agree to give a lecture. Once he was onboard, I lined up the community room in our local library. Then I notified the health reporter at the local newspaper, and she agreed to write a feature article publicizing the event.

On the day of the lecture, my mother and I arrived at the library early and stood in the empty community room. All of a sudden, I wondered what I was doing. What if nobody else showed up?

Instead of anxiously watching the clock, I walked over to the nonfiction section and browsed through a book of quotations.

Words by the poet W. H. Auden caught my eye: "We are all here on earth to help others; what on earth the others are here for I don't know."

Of all the passages I could have found that afternoon, this was the one I was meant to find. I repeated the quote in my mind as I walked back to the community room and peered in the window. To my amazement, while I had been gone, the room had filled with dozens of people, row after row of heads, mostly female. I could see their earrings and scarves, the glint of light on their eyeglasses.

So I wasn't alone, after all.

A thought, then a wish, then a plan, and now here was this concrete reality, a room of living, breathing people.

A feeling welled up in me—one I hadn't experienced since I'd become sick—a swell of satisfaction, optimism, and purpose.

At that moment, the organization that would be the root of my salvation and the answer to my mother's question was born.

Two

LOVE, UNCONDITIONALLY

L upus is primarily a disease of women. Ninety percent of suf-
ferers are female, between the ages of fifteen and forty-four.
Ruby and I both fit within this spectrum, though in other ways we
couldn't have been less alike.

I was a sheltered Jewish high school student when I began the
lupus support group of which she was a member; Ruby was
African-American, and, like the others in the group, old enough
to be my mother. She was also part of a long marriage to a bus
driver named Joe, a bald, heavyset man who accompanied her to
our group each week, still dressed in his uniform.

Ruby was in the end stages of lupus, when the disease caused
inflammation and tissue damage. It had become difficult for her to
dress, button her coat, walk, or even stand. In fact, except for our
meetings, she no longer left the house. But she was there each
Thursday, a reliable fixture sitting in the left corner of the floral
sofa, her husband Joe's big arm around her shoulder. Tall and digni-
fied, in one of her satiny dresses, her hunched posture and swollen
hands were the only signal of how ill she was.

My own experience with lupus had managed to arrest my development in some areas, while maturing me in others. In our group, I was a high schooler advising women my mother's age on handling the vicissitudes of illness—how to obtain transportation, choose a doctor, stand up for themselves in a medical setting.

But when the women began to discuss their personal relationships—the behaviors, problems, and heartaches involving their husbands and children, my advice came to an end.

Being ill so young had thrown a wrench in my social development. I'd yet to have a date, let alone a boyfriend. The one dance I'd attended, big-shoed and ungainly from my swollen feet and the impact of my meds, my friends had to bribe a boy to dance with me and even then I'd stepped on his toes.

Being ill challenges your sense of self; it disrupts the very core of who you are. Like me, the women in the support group suffered from a syndrome similar to post-traumatic stress. Physical pain was only one component of lupus; the emotional consequences were just as complex.

I'm so worried about the future. I don't know how I'm going to afford my medication. I'm not sure how long I can keep my job.

I often sat silent, a teenager absorbing their worries. Even when I had no advice, I came to appreciate the power of listening—of how valuable it can be in connecting and bonding with others.

I learned this from Ruby, who showed great sensitivity in reading other people's moods and emotions. She listened with such love and intensity, nodding her head, extending her hand. And there was something about the way she and Joe sat together that was so compelling. No matter who was talking, I found myself gazing at them.

Yet I knew Ruby's gentle, encouraging way masked her own painful challenges. One evening, after the other group members had left, I went to the window and saw that she was still inching down the driveway, Joe's arm wrapped tightly around her.

Our hostess came up and joined me at the window. "Her heart's failing," she told me. "It's just a matter of time."

I was well aware that lupus can cause a dramatically increased risk of heart disease—from infection to inflammation—and that younger women especially may have a five- to tenfold increased risk compared to the general population.

But those were statistics, and this was Ruby—I turned from the window; there were still some facts I couldn't allow myself to contemplate.

OUR NEXT GROUP SESSION was on the night of my sixteenth birthday. In the past, birthdays had been only minor occasions, marking a mere year in what I'd always assumed would be a long and healthy life. But since my illness, they'd become freighted with new meaning. There's always a clock ticking underneath our lives, but with chronic illness, the tick becomes more audible. I was genuinely moved by the homemade cheesecake crowded with candles, the gifts and cheer of this circle of women who had become my close confidantes and friends. Over the months they'd provided me with the solace I'd once found in rowing—camaraderie, a shared purpose, and a deep sense of connection.

In the crowd of celebrants, I began opening presents.

"Who is this from?" I asked, holding up a handknit sweater.

"Oh, that's from Ruby. Joe brought it over the other day," a friend told me. "She was too sick to come."

The festive mood suddenly vanished. I felt terrible that I hadn't noticed her absence.

"I'd better call her," I said, getting up and going to the phone. But by the time we got through, I learned that Ruby had already been hospitalized and was in organ failure. By the next day, she was gone.

I was astonished to receive a phone call the following evening from Ruby's daughter, asking me to speak at her funeral.

"Are you serious? Why do you want me?"

"My mother thought a lot of you," the daughter said. "She really admired you for starting the group."

"I admired her."

She laughed. "Well, you were a mutual admiration society."

I reluctantly agreed to speak, though I had no idea what I could say that would adequately honor her.

In the Jewish religion mourning is a solemn occasion—with darkened mirrors and days of sitting shiva. So I was unprepared for the jubilant organ music and beaming faces I encountered when I entered the AME Zion church where Ruby's funeral was being held.

I stepped into the church as an elderly woman wearing a straw hat began dancing in the back aisle, a look of joy on her face.

Up front, the altar was crowded with lilies and roses. A choir was positioned up and down the pulpit stairs, swaying and singing: "Oh, happy day!"

This was a celebration—I was obviously in the wrong room.

As I turned to leave, a slim woman in her twenties rushed up and introduced herself as Ruby's daughter.

"You're probably not used to this," she said, seeing my face.

"I wasn't expecting everyone to seem so . . . happy."

"We're celebrating because Mother's with Jesus. She's not suffering anymore."

My grief must have temporarily blinded me; all at once I noticed the white coffin amid the lilies and roses up front and who was beside it—Joe, his head bowed, sitting next to his wife in the same way he had so many times on the couch.

Then I realized what had captivated me about Ruby and Joe—their old-fashioned devoted love, the likes of which I'd rarely witnessed growing up in my family. My parents were two opposing forces who never seemed to mesh, their fractious marriage dominated by scenes of discord and accusation. Their union had shown me exactly what I didn't want in my future, but had also left me bereft of a model to aspire to myself.

As I walked over to offer Joe my condolences, his profile pierced me: This is what I want, I thought; a love like this. Someone who would stand by me in my happiest and my darkest hours, who would be with me right until the end.

OVER THE YEARS, without quite realizing it, I kept Ruby and Joe in my mind's eye until I finally met my husband, Leo. From our first meeting one night at a party, there was a sense of great kindness, an inevitability and ease.

Although my husband could not look less like Joe, there have been times during our marriage, when he's spent hours with me in an emergency room or by my hospital bed, when something about his steadfastness reminds me of my old friend's husband. And I am grateful all over again that I finally found a model to fashion my own image of married life: love that is a solace and a haven.

Three

BREAKING BARRIERS

When I was growing up, our neighbors owned a German shepherd named Duke. The day they brought him home, they took him out on a leash to show him the perimeters of the yard, then set about training him to remain within his boundaries. They circled the yard saying "no" to all the places he wasn't permitted to venture. It took less than a week before he was indoctrinated to remain in the boundaries of their lawn.

Duke stood like a sentinel when my neighbors went out in the street to play baseball. Whenever the ball sailed into his vicinity, he leapt up and caught it in his mouth, then dashed about, tail high in triumph. But whenever the ball crossed the boundary or bounced into the street, he remained frozen, his anguished gaze tracing the ball's forbidden path. There were no fences, electric devices, or leashes to hold him. Yet as desperately as he wanted to run for the ball, he always skidded to a stop, never daring to trespass the perimeters. It was as though he were held back by an invisible force.

Most of us are like my neighbor's dog. Once shown our limits, we abide by them for the rest of our lives. We don't have fences, alarms, or leashes, yet we manage to hold ourselves back with great effectiveness.

AFTER I FOUNDED my lupus support group, during my sophomore year of high school, and discovered the support I needed, my mother assumed I'd fold up my tent and retreat into my own life again. But something my mother had said when I first became ill had still been working on me.

When I was first diagnosed, lupus was all I could see.

"Why me?" I kept asking my mother. I compared my hard fate with the luck of others. I ranted and cried and complained. But the more I coiled up in anger, the deeper my feelings of helplessness and despair.

Then my mother suggested something that seemed both astounding and absurd: that I might have become ill for a reason—that the key might be asking not "What about me?" but "What about others?"

This was a simple but profound shift I would have never experienced without my support group, without those hours sitting in a living room in Atlantic City, listening to women who, like me, were fighting this puzzling, painful battle. They were double and triple my age but still, they knew what it was like to have an immune system attack healthy cells and tissues instead of fighting off foreign intruders.

Even though I was in and out of the hospital, the support group grew, and so did my mission. But I began to envision a new personalized service, where people could contact me not just if they had lupus, but any health problem. My idea was to connect each person with a friend who not only had the same illness but who was also the same age with similar symptoms, lifestyle effects, attitudes, and even hobbies and interests.

When I decided to put my idea into action, friends asked me, "How can you possibly link people all over the country? You don't have any connections." They insisted that there were barriers all around me, but I didn't see them. And since there was no map for me to follow, I made my own path, one step at a time.

WHEN I RECEIVED a scholarship to Rutgers University, I turned leadership of the lupus support group over to its most active member and switched my focus to my new idea, which I called Friends' Health Connection. I began working out of my dorm room in New Brunswick, New Jersey, at age seventeen, during my freshman year of college.

At the time, I didn't know anything about marketing or public relations. So I wrote a very heartfelt letter describing my plan for a national patient support network, then headed to my college library and researched media outlets throughout the country.

I bought boxes of envelopes and made copies of my letter. Each day between classes I addressed letters to top reporters at major newspapers, magazines, and television stations nationwide.

Within a week, I'd received a call from a writer at *USA Today* who said he had simply been touched by my letter and planned to print an article; later, Christiane Amanpour of CNN called me, expressing enthusiasm for my idea, and came to interview me in my dorm room. I was thrilled.

After the article ran and the segment played on Thanksgiving Day, I was bombarded with letters from people suffering from breast cancer, HIV, and rare disorders I'd never heard of before—eye tumors, osteomalacia, femoral neuropathy. Who knew there were so many maladies of the body? Who knew so many others also felt desperate and alone?

Envelopes piled at my feet, postmarked Florida, Oregon, Guam, my name and address scrawled in pen and Magic Marker. Tucked inside each was a person's story, cast out like a message in a bottle.

Suddenly, there was no time to be sick; I had a purpose.

ALL OF US are conditioned to live within a limited perception of our consciousness and power, yet we each have the ability to free ourselves.

Whenever I am about to give a speech or do something that feels a little frightening, I think of my neighbor's dog, who lived and died standing obediently in his tiny square of yard.

It was true that he never escaped or was hit by a car, but he was never able to really run—or live—either.

Four

LISTENING IS LOVE

The first time I started dialysis, my mother and I were visiting my aunt and uncle in northern New Jersey. At nineteen, I'd already had lupus for several years and I knew my kidneys were failing, but I still wasn't yet fully aware of how it was going to impact my life.

On that visit, we'd planned to shop and eat out at local restaurants, but instead I found myself draped across the couch, listless and nauseated. My legs were swollen and I had a terrible headache that wouldn't go away. When I stopped eating, my mother knew I was in trouble and took me to the local hospital.

After a number of tests, the doctor came into the examining room and said to me, "You're going to have to start dialysis right away. Your kidney function's severely compromised."

Normally dialysis is performed through a port surgically implanted in the arm or through a catheter inserted into the peritoneal cavity of the abdomen. But there wasn't time for that. The doctor's plan was to insert a needle into my chest and place a temporary port there. I was rushed into an operating suite and, in a haze of half-consciousness, watched as they implanted the port and connected a bag at my side that filled with bloody fluid.

My mother and I had to remain in the area for the time being in order to be near the hospital. Because we didn't want to intrude on my aunt and uncle, we rented a room in the home of a woman who had the only immediate vacancy we could find. The owner had recently lost her husband.

When we arrived with our belongings, we found that, in the custom of the Jewish religion, the woman's mirrors were covered, and heavy velvet curtains blocked light from the rooms. In a matter of days, our lives had been turned upside down. We were in another town, sequestered in the house of a mourning stranger. I felt like an invalid, frail and unsure.

Over the course of a week I was trained by nurses to self-administer dialysis. In order to stay alive, I had to hook myself up to a portable dialysis machine several times a day.

I was profoundly uncomfortable with dialysis—the very idea of it scared and repulsed me. The first time I performed the procedure on myself in our little room, I fainted and woke to find my mother screaming and calling an ambulance.

Back at the hospital, I met a middle-aged woman who was the wife of a local minister. She'd been on dialysis for many years and treated it with the matter-of-factness of an old veteran.

I told her I couldn't get used to the idea that my body was filling with poisons while other people's kidneys were effortlessly filtering and cleansing their blood.

"You poor thing, you'll get used to it," she told me. "Diabetics need insulin—we need this. Here's my number; if you have any trouble, please call me. I'm an expert at all this by now."

I still felt terrified when I returned to our little room with the machine, bags, and needles. How would I ever handle this on my own? After a fretful night, I decided to take the woman up on her offer.

She was over within the hour and sat beside me, a comforting presence in her tweed suit and cloud of Emeraude cologne. It wasn't so much what she showed me about the machine or needles. It was the way she listened to my fears, which flowed out of me like liquid. How can I do this several times every day? Why did this happen to me? Does this really mean I'm going to die?

Even though there were no answers to some of these questions, she let me ask them. She provided just what I needed—support and an image of survival that were vital.

IN HIS BOOK *Opening Up: The Healing Power of Expressing Emotions*, the psychologist James Pennebaker writes about how healthy and liberating it is to share emotions—to open up and get things off one's chest—not just for the soul, but for immune function and psychological wellness.

"The tendency when overwhelmed is to ruminate, obsessing on just one or two concerns and losing sight of the big picture," Pennebaker writes. "We literally get stuck, bogged down by the weight of a single emotion like anger or sadness or whatever it is we're troubled by."

That's exactly what had happened to me, and what the minister's wife helped banish. In fact, I started my support group and Friends' Health Connection because of how I felt in those dark days of my early illness—because I recognized just how much I needed support.

In that little room where my mom and I temporarily stayed, I was not only surrounded by dialysis equipment, I was also encircled by letters from people who were feeling just as I had. I continued my organization from wherever I was, be it my dorm room, dialysis clinic, or hospital bed.

I extracted patients' stories from the letters they sent me, wrote key criteria on index cards, and filed them in an old Dewey Decimal card storage drawer I salvaged from the local library before it was taken away in the trash. Whenever a new person contacted me, I took out the index cards with information about people who had the same diagnosis and then hand-matched them on a customized, one-to-one basis as closely and carefully as I could.

This system was antiquated, but with the help of fellow college students whom I enlisted to volunteer, thousands of people around the country were successfully matched and many became close confidants and friends.

In starting Friends' Health Connection, I had become a kind of matchmaker of the spirit; people weren't marrying from my connections but finding soul mates who shared the same health problems. Two young men suffering from brain tumors were calling each other every morning for sustenance and encouragement. A woman with cystic fibrosis on the East Coast had bonded with another woman, similarly afflicted, a thousand miles to the west. One member even named her baby in honor of her friend.

What was at the root of this deep, essential connection? It wasn't physical touch—many of these people never laid eyes on one another.

It was something more, something invisible. There's no doubt about it—listening is an act of love.

This wasn't simple listening, the way a clerk hears your description of the kind of shirt you want, but the kind of deep listening similar to the call and response of gospel choirs. One person sings out her pain and trouble and another responds. "Yes, I hear you, I know what you mean." It's a song.

I was reminded of the power of listening again one Mother's Day after my mother died. I was desolate and felt like hiding under the covers all day, but I knew that this wouldn't help. Even huddled under my quilt, my pain would still be with me. So I decided to get up and find something to do that would be a tribute to my mother.

I drove to a local party store, where I bought a dozen helium balloons in a variety of colors and put them in the hatchback of my car. Then I headed to the children's unit of my local hospital. At the nurses' station, I told them my idea. "I'd like to cheer up a sick child. Do you have any suggestions?"

The nurse said there was one girl named Sara who especially needed company. She was alone in room three.

When I knocked on the door, a small voice said, "Come in."

Inside I found an African-American girl around eight years old with large solemn eyes, seated alone in the middle of a bed in an otherwise empty room, no cards, no stuffed animals.

"Hi, Sara," I said, walking in.

"Hello," she said evenly.

"I've brought you some balloons."

She nodded, studying me.

I'd expected a different response—a squeal of childish delight or at least a smile—but this girl wasn't delivering.

"Why're you handing out balloons?" she asked after a few moments.

I sat down on the edge of the bed. "My mother died last year and I wanted to do something to commemorate her."

"How'd she die?"

"Lung problems. She had severe asthma."

Sara nodded again, still studying me. "My sister has asthma."

As she kept asking me questions I found myself telling her more than I'd expected. I talked about my mother's illness and death, about my lupus and kidney transplant, about my fears and sorrow.

Finally I stopped myself. I hadn't intended to go on like this. It was as if I were talking to an adult.

As Sara began telling her story, I understood why. She had recently lost her own mother to AIDS and was HIV positive herself. She basically lived in the hospital; tutors came each week, bringing her books and homework. Her father had left the family years before, and her sister, who had drug problems, only visited occasionally.

Sara reported all this openly, as if her misfortunes were nothing out of the ordinary.

I sat with her for a long while. I had no expert wisdom or advice, and she didn't seem to expect it. Basically, I simply listened.

Eventually I looked at my watch. I hadn't even taken off my coat, and well over an hour had already passed. "I almost forgot about the balloons. What color would you like?"

She looked them over. "I don't know—I can't decide."

"Why don't you take them all," I said, and finally she favored me with a small smile. "I'm really glad I met you today, Sara," I said as I handed over the bouquet of balloons.

"Me too."

By the time I left her room and walked to my car, I felt lighter, my self-pity gone. One balloon was still in the hatchback of my car and I let it escape, watching it ascend into the blue sky over the parking lot.

In a perfect world, Sara would have been looking out of her window, waving at me, but she wasn't.

What had happened in that room, anyway? Sara was still in the hospital—we still mourned our moms. But something powerful had passed between us—a mutual support and understanding that were the foundation of my work and life.

It was nothing visible, yet it was still profound—we had simply taken the time to hear each other.

Five

THE ART OF COMPASSION

One day when I was in elementary school, I was walking with my mother when I noticed a small white butterfly fluttering on the ground.

"What's wrong?" I asked, bending down. "Why isn't it flying?"

My mother leaned closer. "Looks like its wing's torn."

"Can I help it?"

My mother sighed. If anything, I was overly compassionate as a child, always drawn to the broken, the injured, the ones on the margin. "I don't know, Roxanne. You can try, but the wings are very delicate."

That was enough for me. I gingerly picked it up and put it in a lidless shoe box on our screened-in porch. Then I lugged out our *Encyclopaedia Britannica* and began my research. It turned out that my specimen was a clouded sulfur and survived on mud, sap, dew, and rotting fruit. I gave it an old banana and a bowl of water.

Over the next few days, I sat, watching it heal. This seemed to take forever, which was worrisome, given that the encyclopedia had noted that the sulfur's life span was only two or three weeks.

Finally, a few days later, after several attempted liftoffs and the occasional hop and flutter, it flew away into the oak trees of our backyard, and I was left to locate other lost and injured creatures.

My compassion for the suffering of others was part of my impetus for forming Friends' Health Connection. Occasionally, I became so personally embroiled in someone's life and problems that the person's index card stayed with me for months.

That's what happened with a teenage girl named Molly who called me weekly from a small town in Kentucky. Molly had Hodgkin's disease, a cancer that originates in the lymphatic system.

Because Hodgkin's and its treatment affect the body's ability to fight infection, Molly was discouraged from going out in public except for doctor's appointments. She was no longer able to attend school, and spent most of her days alone, homebound in her divorced mother's apartment.

I was eighteen, still in the throes of my own illness, and listening to her talk about her isolation sounded like an echo of my own struggles. Her loneliness was so visceral that I could feel it—a gray miasma that floated through the phone.

One afternoon, she sounded particularly desolate. "I know I'm not supposed to go out in public, but I went to the mall today just to be around other people," she told me.

I knew all too well what it was like to be homebound, lonely, and isolated. The image of her roaming a shopping mall pierced my heart.

"How would you like it if I flew out to see you?" I asked her impulsively.

"Are you kidding! I'd love it," she exclaimed.

She was thrilled by my offer, but no one else thought it was a good idea, particularly my mother.

"You don't even know this girl," she told me. "You can't personally visit everyone who contacts you. You're ill too."

All these things were true. I'd recently been told that my kidney function was deteriorating, and I'd been in and out of the hospital myself. But I was eighteen, old enough to make my own foolish decisions, and so I flew out to Kentucky.

Molly was a slender girl who wore a curly brunette wig, since she'd lost most of her hair. Radiation and chemotherapy had left her looking pale and exhausted, but her face lit up when I arrived.

I decided to take my cues from her and do whatever she felt up for. Her great desire was to sit with me and watch MTV's *Real World,* a reality show that focuses on the lives of strangers who live together in a house—not unlike what the two of us were doing.

Molly was transfixed by these characters, with their health problems, eating disorders, and broken hearts. It was as if by peeking into the plotlines of others, she was participating in life herself.

The other thing Molly wanted to do was talk. She seemed nearly starved for attention and conversation. So I sat beside her, drinking Coke and eating popcorn, absorbing her words like a sponge.

As she spoke, I gained a renewed appreciation for the importance of friendship and support. I knew that I was only one person. But I returned home with a reinforced determination to grow my organization and ensure that no one had to battle illness alone. At the same time, I had to tackle my own health challenges.

As I underwent more tests, the doctors told me I was facing kidney failure. I was scheduled for a biopsy to determine if my kidneys were scarred or inflamed. If they were scarred, I would have to start dialysis and would eventually require a kidney transplant. If they were inflamed then, ironically, like Molly, I might need to undergo a form of chemotherapy to try to save them.

For a brief period, I wandered my college campus, wondering whether I would lose my hair and become like Molly—weak and homebound. I knew we had much in common, but I never dreamed that my life might possibly become an echo of hers.

In the end, it turned out that I didn't need chemo, but a transplant—which sounded to me like a very serious procedure. I had my own challenging road ahead.

Even as I struggled with my illness, the letters kept pouring in—thousands of people just like Molly, who weren't just ill, but also frightened and lonely and often from families as fractured as mine.

In the constellation of my family life, I'd always been aligned with my mother. My father lived with us in the early years in East Paterson, New Jersey, where I was born, but he was a minor character, the only male presence among four females.

His loving acts always seemed the result of my mother's pressure: the doll with long brown curls and pink taffeta dress that he gave me one Hanukkah? Yes, it was beautiful. But I also knew that my mother had locked him out of the house until he'd brought me a suitable gift.

What my father and my mother did best together was fight—doors were slammed and voices raised. What it was all about, I was never certain. Whenever my parents became too loud, my older sisters were expert at shuttling me off into my bedroom and closing the door.

When my parents split apart, I was in the second grade. My father visited, but it was perfunctory and resulted in more arguments. So what was so wrong with him? Everything, according to my mother.

He was a pack rat who collected stacks of papers and hoarded so much junk that we had to carve paths through the maze.

His car was so filled with random trash—boxes, papers, and bicycle wheels—that my mother wouldn't allow him to park it near the house. She was ashamed of him, and I followed suit, taking my cues from her. Obviously he valued stuff over us, his family.

My father had his own story, of course, but I was unable to see it—to see him, as a separate person, apart from his role as my failed parent.

But following my mother's sudden death, there I was in my mid-twenties with my father the surviving parent. For the first time my mother wasn't there, telling me how to feel about him.

After he fell ill himself and moved to an assisted-living facility, I began to visit him regularly and have long talks with him about his own perspectives and life experiences.

It was at this late date that I finally began to understand my father. As a child of the Depression, he'd grown up with so little as a boy that material objects gradually came to symbolize security. I began to see that his hoarding was most likely an obsessive-compulsive disorder that had developed over the years and had never been diagnosed or treated.

Although he hadn't been a great parent, he had many other admirable qualities. He'd spent his working life teaching math and business in the Bronx. Even after his school became violent and he was attacked at gunpoint, he stayed on, never missing a day. In this and many other ways, he was far from a horrible man.

During one of those visits, I thought of the life cycle of that butterfly I'd been so fascinated with as a child—the way it was laid out in the *Encyclopaedia Britannica:* the egg, the larva, the chrysalis, the butterfly, the short, but perfect circle. I'd been more aware of the cycle of that two-winged creature than the journey of my own father, who had labored under injuries and tribulations of his own.

Sometimes those who need the most compassion are right beside us, but they are obscured by their roles, by our own expectations of them and disappointments about our relationship with them. My father'd had his own struggles, and mine had finally made me more sympathetic.

My visits with my father continued over the next several years as his health deteriorated. Finally, several of his organs began to fail and he suffered a minor heart attack.

His doctor called and told me, "He's not going to last much longer." So I got in my car and drove the two hours' distance to reach his bedside.

I was able to sit next to him throughout the night, watching the monitors around his room as they beeped and hummed. As he passed early in the morning, I whispered to him, "Thank you for all the good you've done," and in my heart, a long-frozen region finally thawed.

Six

DRIVING LESSONS

H ere is how I learned how to drive:

One afternoon when I was sixteen I was riding beside my mother as she careened her way through the streets of Manhattan. We were in midtown, in the midst of the densest, tensest traffic imaginable: streams of taxis, bicycle deliverymen, street vendors hawking their wares, pedestrians darting out at intersections.

None of this fazed my mother. It was as if she had a kind of traffic Zen that allowed her to flow through the chaos. She used her horn like a little staccato bell, ignoring hand gestures and shouts from the drivers around us. She dodged and swerved through traffic, managing to catch almost all the green lights on our trip down Broadway.

Meanwhile, on my side of the car, I was drenched with the special anxiety of the uninitiated. I had never driven myself, but that didn't keep me from mashing down on imaginary brakes, gripping the door handle, and gasping, "Watch out! Slow down!"

"Relax, Roxanne," my mother said as she merrily wove along. "Have I ever failed you?"

Well, she had a point: she was a terrible driver in so many ways, easily distracted, always switching lanes and missing exits. But somehow, we always got where we were going.

"I don't know how you can drive in this," I muttered at one point when we were gridlocked between an EMT ambulance and a vegetable truck.

There was a moment of silence and I realized I'd made a terrible mistake. My mother had been threatening to give me driving lessons for months now, but we hadn't found the right time or place. It was just this kind of comment that she could easily turn into a challenge.

As she pulled over to the side of the street, my heart sank. I'd done it.

"C'mon. This is a good place for you to learn."

"Oh, Mom, not here!"

"Yes, it's perfect."

We both got out of our respective sides, ignoring the honking traffic around us, and made the switch.

I buckled my seat belt, sweat pouring down my back.

Before me was a complex knot of buses, lights, signs, police cars, tourists—everything vying for my attention. I was on the corner of Fiftieth Street and Broadway, in what seemed the center of the vehicular world.

"Okay, you've got to put yourself out there," my mother instructed. "Don't be timid—no one will ever let you in if you are!"

I gripped the wheel as if it were a life preserver and inched the car out into traffic as slowly as an armored tank, to a hail of honks.

"Ignore them. You can do it. Just keep going."

I lurched and swerved my way along Fiftieth, heading east. As I did so, I realized there was something familiar about this experience.

My mother and I had moved from Allentown, Pennsylvania, to Atlantic City, New Jersey, when I was ten. Being raised in Atlantic City, I had grown up in the ocean. While other girls stood at the edge of the surf, screaming and cringing, I threw myself into the cold churning waters like a sea creature. It was where I felt at home.

Yet there was always a point during my daily swims when I was confronted with a frightening obstacle. I'd look up and find myself facing a huge wave coming right at me. It was always a dilemma. I knew I could never run fast enough to escape the wave, yet I couldn't remain still or it would overtake me. My only choice was to hold my breath, dive right into it, and keep swimming, until I eventually ended up where the water's rise and fall was gentle and serene.

That was exactly what happened that day in Manhattan.

Twenty minutes after I had slid behind the wheel, I'd reached the east side of the island, facing the East River and an area of calm. I had crossed Fifth, Park, Madison, Lexington, Second, and First. Along the way I'd encountered a fender bender and a manhole construction site, and I just missed a skateboarder who'd darted out from between two parked cars.

"There," my mother said with satisfaction as I pulled over. "Nothing will ever be that hard again."

Well, that was true—in terms of traffic. I was never frightened of driving after that. But in terms of my illness, my fearlessness would be put to the test over the years in a number of ways I couldn't have imagined then.

I WAS LEARNING to drive during the same years I was learning to live with lupus—and there were parallels.

There are two ways of being a patient—you can be meek and docile or fierce and bold. Like most patients, I began the first way—following in the doctors' wake like a small, obedient animal. Whatever they said, no matter how difficult it was, I complied without question, just as I'd passively waited in traffic.

No more sun? Okay, I would dutifully stay in the shade, although being outdoors in the middle of the day was my favorite activity in the world.

Take massive doses of steroids? Fine, even though they left me swollen and bloated, and caused me to lose much of my hair.

My mother was the nurse, so in the beginning, it was natural to leave the questioning to her.

In fact, she was the one who insisted early on in my lupus diagnosis, when I was fifteen, that I be given a closed kidney biopsy, an outpatient procedure performed through the skin. The alternative, an open biopsy, involved major surgery, general anesthesia, and a longer recuperation period.

Still, it was frightening enough: the insertion of a long thin needle into my kidney and the extraction of a tissue sample. I hated needles, so I was plenty terrified the morning of the procedure. My mom followed my stretcher as I was transported through the hospital halls.

As we neared the biopsy room, I saw two doctors conferring, their heads bowed together.

They looked up as we entered: I was shocked by the face of the younger doctor. He was pale and looked a little ill himself, as well as extremely nervous. A description floated into my mind: green around the gills. It fit him exactly.

There is a powerlessness, a loss of dignity that often accompanies hospital life. Stripped of your identity, placed in inmate clothes, you become a body that any stranger can touch, poke, and prod. Interns arrive when you're lying half-naked, students study your body as if it were a quiz. Some of this is inevitable, but in my short span as a patient, I had begun to see how important it was to try to preserve part of one's self.

That afternoon, something rose to the surface that surprised even me.

"Which one of you is doing my procedure?" I asked once I was situated on the table, looking up at two men in white coats.

The younger one raised his hand as if he were a schoolboy.

"Would you mind telling me how many times you've done this before?"

"Roxanne!" my mother said, appalled. As a nurse, she had been trained never to directly confront a doctor.

"Well, I want to know," I said, undeterred, still staring at the young doctor. "You look nervous, and I'm not having this biopsy done by someone who isn't experienced."

The younger doctor was all watery blue eyes—he looked as if he wanted to flee the room.

The older doctor stepped up. "Never mind, I'll do it. He can watch."

The older doctor talked me through the procedure, as I'd requested. The needle was to be inserted through my back and into my kidney. He numbed the biopsy site and it took less than a minute for the needle to enter and come out again. I felt pressure, but no intense pain. The most frightening part was the click and pop sound that the needle made as it clamped the biopsy sample.

When it was over, the older doctor left the room, but the younger one stayed behind. He removed his surgical mask and looked down at me.

"Actually, I was very nervous. You would have been my first patient for this procedure."

He shook my hand, and my mother and I watched him walk away.

"I was mortified, but you were right," she said after a moment.

My mother had taught me to be fierce but she wasn't always pleased with my execution. That's the thing about teaching someone a lesson; you have no control over how they'll eventually use it.

I DID NOT ALWAYS heed my mother's lessons—either in the car or out in the world.

When she told me once, as part of her driving instruction, that I should honk every time I approached an intersection and others would halt, I knew she was wrong.

But I took many of her larger lessons to heart, and I'm glad I did. I lost her as my champion far sooner than I ever imagined and I had to become an advocate for myself.

Even now, years after her death, whenever I find myself in a daunting intersection, I think of that day in Manhattan, and the mere thought of her beside me makes me gather my courage and press down even harder on the gas.

Seven

THE GRACE OF GRATITUDE

After my mother died, my two older sisters became the carriers of my childhood stories, the repository of anecdotes from when I was a girl.

My sister Wendy told me that when I was in elementary school, I was so entranced with Superman that I kept making her take me to see the movie and even announced that I was going to marry Christopher Reeve one day.

But what Wendy didn't realize was that I didn't just want to marry Superman, I wanted to be him.

I had just finished second grade and was desperate to escape our new life in Allentown, Pennsylvania, where my mother and I had moved after she'd broken up with my dad.

It wasn't simply that I was separated from my beloved sisters, who at twenty-three and twenty-four had remained behind in East Paterson, but my mother had placed me in a private school full of wealthy strangers whose parents were lawyers and doctors, who had butlers and live-in maids. They owned homes with porticos, pillars, and winding driveways; in comparison, our little town house could have been a garage.

During my first week in this alien environment, there was a mysterious infestation. My classmates and I were called into the health office to have our scalps checked under special lights. A gloved nurse separated my strands of hair with a wooden stick, then announced in a loud voice: "Black, Roxanne—lice!" I was sent home, along with several other students, but it felt as if I were the only one.

I was horrified that there were parasites in my long, brown hair, nits that required human blood to live. It made me feel dirty and reinforced the sense that I was out of place in this wealthy school.

My mother went into a frenzy of cleaning, vacuuming our worn carpet and washing everything in boiling water. But by the time I returned to school, the damage had been done. No one would come near me except to taunt or punch me. To my mother's alarm, I came home with long blue bruises on my legs and arms. She called the school to complain, but it made no difference. Eventually, I stopped telling my mother what was happening and found ways to cope on my own, creating elaborate fantasies, using Superman as a guide.

I imagined bursting out of my school clothes, emerging in my own blue body suit, flashing through the air to fight back the villains who mocked me. I savored their shock when they realized that mild Roxanne Black, shy and teased, actually had a powerful secret identity.

But mostly, I dreamed of flying; of lifting my skirt and sailing over the treetops, back to the cul-de-sac in East Paterson, New Jersey, where I'd once been the sheltered and adored youngest child.

I thought of all these superpower fantasies decades later, on the day I met Christopher Reeve in person. That was the day I accompanied a local newspaper reporter to his home in a rural area of Westchester County, New York.

The reporter was writing about an upcoming lecture that Christopher Reeve was going to give for my organization. Several years after I started Friends' Health Connection, I added an ongoing lecture series that features leaders in health, wellness, and motivation. In addition to connecting individuals with the same health challenges, I wanted to provide access to expert speakers whose knowledge and experience could help people live healthier lives. Christopher Reeve was one of our speakers.

When the reporter and I arrived for the interview, we were directed to his room at the end of a long corridor. As I began to walk down it, I spotted him there in the distance, stationary in the center of a sun-filled room.

I had already been inspired by Reeve's heroic story. Weeks after he'd become a quadriplegic from the spinal cord injuries he suffered when his horse pitched him headlong onto the ground, he'd begun advocacy work, fighting to increase public awareness about spinal cord injuries and raising money for a cure.

Yet when he'd first regained consciousness and realized that he was paralyzed from the neck down, he later wrote that he wasn't even certain he wanted to live. "Maybe we should just let me go," he told his wife, Dana. "I can't live like this."

But she urged him to take two weeks to think about it, and said that if he still wanted to give up, she would support him. She knew that given a little time, he might change his mind, and he did.

In the end, he decided to take life one day at a time: "There are people who love me and who I love very much. And if they are willing to accept me just the way I am, and are willing to go on this journey with me, well, then, who am I to quit?"

Even though doctors held out no hope that Reeve would ever regain function below the neck, he still dedicated himself to maintaining his body through an intense, five-hour-a-day exercise program, strapped to devices that moved his limbs for him. He fought pneumonia, infections, broken bones, wounds, and blood clots. And for seven years, his body remained motionless.

I knew these facts, but I was unprepared for the sight of Reeve's frozen body as I entered the room, which was silent except for the sound of his breathing, amplified by the ventilator. It was like coming before some great god or wizard who had been completely immobilized.

The reporter took notes as Reeve spoke in a paced, resonant voice about coming to terms with his injury. In his dreams, he said, he was never disabled, but still able to sail, ride horses, and run. Even now, he said, he sometimes felt shock and sorrow when people walked away from him. He had to come to terms all over again with the fact that he was unable to do so himself.

At the time of our visit, for the first time since his accident, Reeve had regained the ability to make a small movement with his index finger on one hand; he was the first patient to have such an improvement years after his initial injury, an unprecedented development.

This small movement was what he focused on now—one movement, of one finger. "If I can move this finger," he asked, "what else can I possibly move?"

I was grateful that I wasn't conducting this interview. I realized that I was sitting with my mouth open, unable to tear my gaze from that face I had studied so intently when I was a lost and lonely girl.

But I was also thinking of my own journey. At that point, I was thirty. Nearly a decade had passed since my sister Bonnie had donated her kidney to me for my first transplant. While I still had to have periodic blood tests, I was otherwise living a normal, energetic life.

Before that transplant, I'd suffered such profound nerve damage in my legs that it felt as if I were walking on hot needles whenever I took a step. The doctors had warned that this damage might be irreversible, and that without a transplant, there was a good chance I would spend the rest of my life in a wheelchair.

After the surgery, Bonnie's kidney began working almost immediately, and the nerve damage quickly reversed itself.

For months afterward, I thought of her whenever I ran, pain free, up a flight of stairs or dashed down a hallway, acts I could never have performed in my frail pre-transplant state.

My years of illness had made me certain that I would always be actively grateful, not just for my health but for my sister's sacrifice—for allowing an organ to be removed from her body, packed in ice, then taken a few yards away into the next room and placed into a new home, in me.

But just enough time had passed for me to take all this for granted, to slide back down the slope of discontent. Lately I had been letting small things bother and distract me—aggravations at work, encounters with people who annoyed me. Why was this report so late? Why didn't he call me back? Why did she look at me that way? Nothing large, just the small, petty grievances that eroded attention from the miraculous fact that I was still alive.

As the interview drew to a close that afternoon, Reeve looked over at me.

"Would you mind adjusting my tube before you go?" he asked, referring to the small straw that he blew into in order to operate his electric wheelchair. Moving it, I was hit with fresh force at how dependent this formerly self-reliant man was on others for his most basic needs.

One movement, of one finger.

As I walked back down that hall into my own life, I thought of the comment Reeve had made earlier about feeling sorrow when people walked away from him, and I wondered if he was watching me and feeling that same way now. But I resisted the temptation to look back and made myself concentrate instead on the marvel of walking—an act, like breathing, that we rarely consider unless we can't do it anymore. I noted how gracefully my leg left the ground and swung forward from the hip, how my two legs coordinated so that one foot or other was always in direct contact with the ground.

There were ninety-seven steps from Reeve's office to the car that day and I savored every one.

Never before had I been so grateful for this simple act. My encounter with Reeve had peeled away my layer of complacency and reminded me how well my body—my old, loyal friend—was still working, propelling me forward after so many years of uncertainty and pain. The sheer luck of my life washed over me. Remember this, I told myself.

As the reporter drove me home, I took out a piece of paper from my purse and decided to make a list, headed: "All I am grateful for."

That February day that had seemed so unremarkable a few hours before was suddenly shot through with grace and beauty—I noticed a golden crocus poked out of a melting snowbank, a flock of returning birds circled overhead.

By the time we pulled into my driveway, I had filled the page with words of thanks.

That interview was the first time I met Christopher Reeve, but it wouldn't be the last. His example would teach me many things over the years. But on that afternoon he reminded me of the living power of gratitude and how the real superpowers were interior ones that reside in all of us—if only we remember to harness them.

Eight

GIVING HOPE

It's ironic that doctors, who provide so much hope for their patients, can also be the ones to snatch it away.

Recently I went looking for a general practitioner who I could see for regular checkups. With my health history, meeting a new doctor is almost like meeting a new therapist—the narrative of my body is long and complex. But it is a story with an upbeat theme, and I was happy to inform the first doctor on my list, a dour, middle-aged man, how well I was feeling.

"We'll see if that continues," he said, writing down numbers, avoiding my eye. "You still have lupus."

When I went on to report my kidney function numbers, which were excellent, he seemed unimpressed and muttered under his breath, "They're fine for now."

And as I began listing my medications, he muttered, "Those drugs are all forms of chemotherapy, you realize."

In fact, whatever I said throughout the appointment, he followed it with a similarly negative, fear-inducing comment. I felt my normal optimism leak away and a force, dark as ink, seep into the room.

In fact, all these comments went without saying. After years of living with lupus, I was well aware of the dark side, but it was the bright side that I needed to focus on.

That doesn't mean that I put my head in a paper bag, ignored treatment advice, or lived in some land of denial. On the contrary, I've been an involved and active patient. But I also hold on to something inside myself that isn't evident on any PET scan or MRI.

Dr. Jerome Groopman, an oncologist who has written about the power of hope in surviving illness, has commented that he wished he had a nickel for every patient he knew who was told he was incurable but was now doing fine. Groopman also notes something I've personally discovered—that there is often a cure or new treatment just around the corner, so patients shouldn't think in terms of forever.

How many times doctors have given me the grimmest of news and written off my future!

When I was on dialysis before my first transplant, I was told that I would never walk again because toxins had built up in my body and caused severe nerve damage in my feet. Many of my doctors were convinced I was headed toward a wheelchair for the rest of my life.

Yet as soon as I received my transplant, this nerve damage reversed and corrected itself. Within a short time, I walked fine and even took up jogging and tennis.

When my kidneys failed the first time, physicians insisted that I would require a blood transfusion every week for several years until I received a transplant.

But at my following appointment, the very next week, they changed direction and said I wouldn't need even one more transfusion because they had decided to use a new injection that kept blood levels from dropping in patients with end-stage renal function.

Many physicians told me I'd never live a normal life. When I was fifteen, several even told me I might die. In fact, when I was discharged once from the hospital, a clerk wrote "Date of D" on my hospital papers. When these documents were submitted to insurance, this was interpreted as meaning the date of my death. My insurance company informed Social Security that I had passed away.

For years after, I had great trouble proving that I was among the living. My credit report was linked to my Social Security number, so any time I tried to get anything in my name—even a cell phone—my records insisted I was dead.

It took me years to prove to Social Security that there was a mistake. I learned that it can be as difficult to prove you're alive as it is to stay positive in the face of illness.

It's important to hold on to our dream of health and to find others who foster it. Sure, we have to face facts and medical realities. But we also have to preserve a little room all our own, where we tend the fire of our hope and keep it alive.

I had a chance encounter with a doctor years ago who unwittingly helped me do just that.

When my kidneys first began to fail in college, I became severely anemic. My hemoglobin level, which was supposed to be 12, often dropped as low as 5. When this happened I developed difficulty breathing and speaking. During these attacks, one of my college roommates, caring and panicked, would usually drive me, to the emergency room.

On one occasion, in my junior year, I was sitting in a science class when I could feel this happening. The room started to swim—my legs and arms felt as if they belonged to someone else.

I decided to walk over to the local hospital, which was only a few blocks away.

Once I'd arrived and had my blood tested, the nurse came out with a worried look. "Your numbers are really low," she said. "You're going to have to get to Philadelphia right away and be admitted," she added, referring to the kidney center where I was being treated.

I stood up woozily, breaking down all I had to do. The first thing was to reach the elevator, the next was to walk to my apartment and pack a bag.

I couldn't go any further than that.

I was in the midst of making my way to the elevator when I swooned and nearly passed out.

A gray-haired doctor came up to me and took my arm to hold me up.

"Are you okay?"

I told him my situation—why I was there, where I was heading.

"How are you getting home?"

"I'm walking."

"Alone?"

I nodded.

"No, you're not."

I thought he'd look for a nurse or orderly to accompany me. But no.

"C'mon, I'll walk with you," he said.

He wasn't my doctor—I'd never seen him before. Later I would learn that he was one of the senior doctors at the hospital, an esteemed researcher and clinician. But to me, then, he was a compassionate older gentleman who took my arm and escorted me several blocks. I don't remember the walk, but I remember the pressure of his arm, the warm spot in the center of his eyes when he looked over at me—the care there, I could see it.

When I opened my door and thanked him, he put his hand on my shoulder. "It's going to be all right," he said, and here's the thing: I believed him.

Hope—so easy to provide; so devastating to take away.

The address the doctor escorted me to was a dumpy, run-down college apartment I shared with several roommates. The kitchen had a battered hardwood floor that we had covered with an old rug. When I pulled the rug back to clean one day, I noticed that tiny plants had sprouted through the slats. My roommates and I pulled them out and sprayed the slats with weed killer. But no matter what we did, the plants always grew back.

My roommates thought these plants were disgusting, but I was fascinated by their obstinate, vital growth. Under layers of wood, in darkness, these sprigs of green life kept pushing up and breaking through.

There is an impulse to adapt and survive, to preserve our souls and selves that is apparent throughout nature, as alive in humans as in those weeds pushing up through the wood.

I think of hope like those plants: it's hard to snuff out. You need only a little air and light to keep it alive.

Nine

SYNCHRONICITY

Einstein said that there are two ways to live your life—one is as though nothing were a miracle; the other is as if everything is.

I choose the latter way.

My life has been full of synchronicity, lucky turns and twists of fate—a hand extended in assistance at the moment I desperately needed it, love galloping around the corner just in the nick of time.

My cousin Dave once told me, "You know, I was born, made it through childhood, fell in and out of love, went on trips, graduated college, switched jobs—all to be standing on this street corner with you at this very second."

After he said this, we both looked at each other, mindful that all we'd done in our lives had culminated in this instant. Then we blinked, and it was over, and we were back to our rushed unconscious lives.

I often think of fate and coincidence when I enter an elevator and stand pressed close to total strangers, smelling their sweat and aftershave, breathing their same air. Why are we all together in this small box, passing each other at this exact moment in the universe?

My own history, even with its dips and dark valleys, has been full of amazing moments of fortuitous connection. In starting my organization, I was guided by a whole chain of people who appeared one after another to give me help and understanding—starting with my high school principal who allowed me to use the teachers' lounge during my lunch break to make phone calls for my support group, attaining the privacy and quiet I needed during calls with those who were ill—to many other benefactors who took me under their wings and provided support.

I've also witnessed many amazing examples of synchronicity in the people in my life.

I was at the beach with my mother when she was talking about how anxious she was about money. She never seemed to have enough, but that month she was particularly worried about the mortgage. We were in beach chairs, sitting in the shallow surf, and she was waving her hands back and forth in the water as she talked. All of a sudden a dollar bill floated into her hand. Then another and another. As we looked, all kinds of money started washing in with the surf at our feet—five-, ten-, and twenty-dollar bills.

Was it a boating accident? Had someone lost a wallet? We never knew for sure. But that day, just as she was asking for it, money literally floated into my mother's hands.

And then there's my friend Gloria, a hairstylist. By the time she'd reached her early forties she'd managed to start a successful business, save money, and help her family, but her fondest wish—

to have a child—had eluded her. While she had been setting up her life, her biological clock had ticked away and she now found herself childless and bereft.

One day, a weary-looking woman in her twenties appeared in her salon and said she needed a haircut. She slumped into the chair, and as Gloria trimmed her hair, she talked about her life.

It had been a hard one—she was an alcoholic, a recent divorcée with a young son, and she was struggling to survive.

"I've been ordered to go into rehab, and I don't know what I'm going to do with my kid while I'm gone. There's no one I can turn to."

And with that she brought out a photo of an adorable tow-headed boy, and burst into tears.

My friend wasn't sure what possessed her to say the first words that flew into her head: "I'll take care of him until you get out."

"Are you serious?" the woman asked her.

Yes, Gloria said, she was.

She invited the woman to her home, which she had made cozy and inviting for the family she'd never managed to have. She made cookies and there was a fire in the woodstove, her cats curled up on the couch. She met the boy, named Trey, who immediately walked up to her and sat in her lap.

"Do you want to stay here while Mommy gets better?" the mother asked at the end of the evening, after he had stuffed himself with meat loaf and mashed potatoes.

Without aplomb, Trey said that he did.

So the mother went into rehab for three months and emerged, still shaky, still unable to support her son. She visited Gloria and told her, "I really appreciate everything you've done, but I'm still not strong enough to hold down a job. I think Trey should go live with my sister in Texas for a while."

What could Gloria say? She kissed Trey good-bye, noting that he looked every bit as unhappy as she was. In those months, he and Gloria had bonded so intensely that she forgot what her life had been like before this sunny creature, who bloomed under the love she had stored up all those years.

But this woman was his mother, and Gloria had no rights.

That was that, she thought.

One afternoon several months later, the mother was back at Gloria's salon, crying again.

"Trey's miserable. He doesn't like Texas. My sister's over-whelmed with her own kids. I can't take care of him—I don't think I'll ever be able to take care of him—and she can't either."

And then, as in a fairy tale, where things work out in the end as if by magic, where those who love are reunited and truth and beauty win the day, Trey was back with Gloria. Eventually she was able to adopt him, with the mother's blessing.

If that isn't synchronicity, I don't know what is.

DEEPAK CHOPRA spoke for my organization about the law of least effort—the power of sitting back and being guided, taking signs from the universe. Chopra contends that we can do less and ac-complish more. But this is so against our rushed and striving na-tures. We want to be in control, so we grip the steering wheel of our lives. Sometimes, we need to let life guide us, so that we can be brought to the places and people that are meant for us.

I certainly believe this is true when I think of the way I've met many crucial people in my life—and one of them in particular.

There was no obvious reason why I decided at the last minute to go to that New Year's Eve party in 2002. I was looking forward to getting into flannel pajamas and watching the ball drop by myself.

But a friend of mine called at the eleventh hour and implored me to come to her house for a party: "Please come. I just hate for you to be alone on New Year's Eve."

I didn't mind being alone; I was used to it. But something in her voice touched me.

So even though the party was an hour away and required me to get up and get dressed, I agreed to go.

There at the party was a nice-looking guy in his forties, who'd just returned from Texas where he'd been visiting his sister.

There were no bells or sirens. He brought me a plate of lasagna. Then he sat beside me as I played a board game, watching as I rolled the dice and moved my piece around the board.

It was cold and frosty outside, but inside there were lights and laughter. Looking around at the crowd, I was glad that I'd made the effort to come.

I think of that evening now—the dice, my moving pieces, the board laid out in front of us—as if it were a small blueprint of my life.

I didn't know then that this interaction, those few hours with this kind man, would usher in a new future for me and the kind of marriage I had long yearned for but never thought I would find.

Why did I go to this party of all others?

Why did Leo return on that day from his sister in Texas?

These are the questions that cannot be answered by our rational minds.

Einstein said that in order to understand life, we should look into nature.

Sometimes I do just that—stare at a flower that's just opened or watch a bird doing what it was meant to do, flying across the sky.

They do these things because it is in their nature. And human nature, according to Chopra, is to "make our dreams manifest into physical form, easily and effortlessly."

Before my future husband left the party that evening, he went around the room and wished everyone good night.

When he came to me, he kissed my cheek and said, "Happy New Year. Good night, sweetie."

Those words sounded so familiar, so right to me, that I felt a sweet foreboding and had a glimpse of the complex circuitry, the convergence of luck and fate that can come together when we let the universe guide us.

Ten

JUST AS WE ARE

Now, I realize it is one of the oldest plots in the world, but when I was young, the story of my mother, a small-town girl with high hopes, seemed right out of a fairy tale.

Her thwarted singing career was the backstory of my childhood. Both she and my grandmother possessed exquisite voices and longed to be entertainers. My mother was the one who escaped her hometown of Allentown, Pennsylvania, for New York City to follow her dream.

One night at Harlem's Apollo Theater, she had her big break. In a bit of luck right out of the movies, the lead singer came down with the flu and at the last minute my mother was placed in her slot. She was the opening act for Cab Calloway's orchestra and received a standing ovation. Backstage, people clustered around to praise her, and a handsome young producer told her that she was destined to be a star.

But my mother shared another trait with my grandmother—a strong strain of self-doubt and insecurity. By the next week, she was on the bus returning to Allentown. She backed away from success, a lesson that was not lost on her—or me.

As much as I adored my mother, she had a way of continually raising the bar as I was growing up. Whatever I accomplished, there was another level I felt I had to achieve.

When the two of us visited the White House, where I was being honored by President George H.W. Bush for starting Friends' Health Connection, we were both elated and nervous. Tripping on her high heels, dressed in a new suit, she gripped my arm as we walked into the Rose Garden, whispering, "Oh, Roxanne, Grandma would be so proud to know that we're meeting the president." Then she paused, and added, "Maybe next we can meet the pope."

She wasn't kidding. There was always a "but" with her, one more rung that I needed to reach. So I kept dutifully climbing, piling the accolades up behind me, building a fortress of honors and awards.

It started in high school, when I won the Bill Bradley Young Citizens Award, and continued throughout college, when I was designated one of the top eighteen college students in the nation. NBC and CNN sent camera crews to my dorm room and followed me to class. I was honored with a presidential medal and featured in *USA Today* and *The New York Times*.

My mother discovered the art of lamination and followed in my wake, happily preserving my commendations and awards in plastic. Soon there were so many that we could scroll them out, like carpet, on the floor. Yet somehow, I always needed more.

Then, on the eve of my twenty-fifth birthday, I picked up the phone to hear words I could barely register. My mother had been discovered dead from an asthma attack—alone at home. She'd suffered from emphysema and asthma for years, but she'd always downplayed the severity of her symptoms. I was the one with the significant illness.

Since childhood, my mother had been my sidekick, the one who stood vigil at my hospital bed, who clapped in the front row of any audience in which I spoke. Now the wind at my back, my dearest fan and booster had vanished. After my initial disbelief, I was blanketed with sorrow. How could I survive without her? Who would guide me now?

But over the years, my mother's ambitious persona seemed to have set up a permanent base in me. After her death, that voice continued whispering in my ear: "What else?" it asked. "What's next?"

Throughout the rest of my twenties I worked as if possessed, arriving early at my office, and falling asleep with my head on the computer keyboard. I had no social life: friends didn't fit into my frantic schedule, and dates were out of the question.

But, for helping individuals with health challenges all over the country, there were more awards and honors than ever. They hung on my office walls and cluttered my desk, proof that I had weight and value. Without them, without the cloak of work around me, I didn't know how to be myself—I didn't even know who myself was. Somewhere along the way I'd become a work machine, a human *doing* rather than a human *being*.

It was around this time that a roommate invited me to a party for a woman turning fifty. In an attempt to poke fun at her aging, partygoers were instructed to dress up as though they were elderly themselves.

Parties were among the many social settings I avoided, and this one sounded particularly painful.

"I don't want to go, and I definitely don't want to dress up," I told the friend who'd invited me.

"Oh, c'mon, Roxanne—you don't want to go anywhere unless it has to do with work."

She was right, of course. So I capitulated; my friend arrived at my apartment the night of the party with a large bag of paraphernalia. Once we started to dress up, I actually began having fun.

In the past for an event like this, I would have tried hard to look perfect, studying myself from every angle, making sure my hair was in place, my makeup carefully applied. I would have debated what outfit to wear, what shoes and purse.

But this time, I did just the opposite. I made myself look as ridiculous and unattractive as I could. I smeared on turquoise eye shadow and orange lipstick. I tossed my hair, stuck a roller in the middle, and sprayed the whole concoction with gray hair color.

I pulled on a pair of men's pajama bottoms with an oversize striped flannel top and knee-high stockings full of runs. I stuffed my bra with socks so my fake breasts hung low on my chest.

By the time I was done, I barely recognized myself.

In fact, the costume was so elaborate and foreign that it had a liberating effect.

Once at the party, I felt oddly exhilarated by my new persona, protected against all my old haunting insecurities. I was an old woman now, long past the age when I had to worry what anyone thought of me. I approached strangers and started conversations. I told jokes and laughed.

I had always been too self-conscious to dance—but not that night. I followed one guy after another onto the floor and danced with abandon, without that nagging critical voice that was always

murmuring in my head. At one point, I even took the DJ's microphone and began singing. Unlike the other women in my family, I
had a voice like a shriek and could butcher any tune. But that night,
I didn't care.

I had never allowed myself to be spontaneous, to let my hair
down, to simply be as I was, and I was amazed at the result.

I'd rarely been noticed at a party, let alone the star. Now here
I was, baggy-chested with rollers in my hair, and men were swarm-
ing all around me as I sang, danced, and laughed. And none of them
knew a thing about me—there wasn't an honor, an award, or a
newspaper article within miles.

I went into the bathroom and looked at myself, flushed, mussed,
gray hair askew. So here I was, after all, the me of me, buried behind all the rubble. It was ironic that getting in touch with my
inner old lady was what brought my authentic youthful self back
to me.

It wasn't eyeliner or lip gloss, awards or medals. None of that
mattered. It was simply the self I'd possessed all along.

After that, whenever that hectoring voice began chanting her
fearful entreaties—What will people think of me? What if I look
like a fool?—I summoned up my wild and wily alter ego to banish
them. I harked back to that party when I stood, microphone in
hand, singing with abandon, dancing as if no one else were there.

Eleven

ORDINARY COURAGE

I was humbled when I received an award from the Four Chaplains Memorial Foundation, which was established to honor a rabbi, a priest, and two Protestant ministers who were killed during action in World War II.

When the clergymen's army transport ship was hit by a German torpedo in February 1943, it was packed with 902 servicemen, merchant seamen, and civilian workers. The blast killed dozens and seriously wounded many others. Witnesses reported pandemonium, as men jumped into overcrowded lifeboats or were swept into the icy ocean. One witness, who found himself floating with the dead all around him, heard the chaplains preaching courage. "Their voices were the only thing that kept me going," he said.

The chaplains handed out life jackets to the men who were topside. When the life jackets ran out, another witness observed the chaplains remove their own jackets and hand them to four frightened soldiers. The rabbi didn't call out for a Jew, or the priest for a Catholic—the chaplains simply provided their jackets to the next soldiers in line.

As the ship sank, survivors witnessed the chaplains linking arms and praying, braced against the slanting deck as they went down. Of the 902 men aboard the ship, 230 survived.

This is what I always considered courage—magnificent feats of bravery in the face of catastrophic circumstances.

It was only after I became ill that I realized courage can also consist of small daily acts in the midst of ordinary life.

One day, a devastated young husband called my organization about his wife, who'd recently been in a serious car accident. Her car had skidded off the road in icy weather and turned over, causing her severe injuries. She had been airlifted to a special burn unit where a team of specialists worked frantically to save her. Her survival had been a miracle; but in the process, she'd lost a leg.

It was on this loss that the young woman focused. The amputation was so traumatic that she sank into a deep depression and turned away from her husband.

"She's completely withdrawn from me—she won't even allow me to touch her anymore," the man told me. "I still love her as much as ever, but it's like she's stopped living."

The accident wasn't what had torn the couple apart, but the wife's reaction to it. She wasn't able to muster the courage it takes to face the daily challenges of disability and illness. It's not easy.

AFTER MY SECOND KIDNEY TRANSPLANT, my husband and I were anxious to take a vacation. For two years, I'd been on a transplant waiting list, and we'd stuck close to home, never knowing when the phone call would come and I'd be rushed into surgery. We kept our cell phones on all the time, even at the movies, so we could run at any moment.

My first donated kidney—from my sister, Bonnie—had valiantly taken me through thirteen years. With it, I had started Friends' Health Connection, completed college, and mourned my mother. Now, as if worn out by all these events, it had begun to fail. There was no telling how long a kidney transplant might last—I knew a woman who had one for thirty years, and another for only two.

In any case, this second transplant loomed before Leo and me, an event in the middle of our future that we both dreamed of and dreaded.

But once the second surgery was completed and my new kidneys had worked well for nearly a year, we decided it was time to take a vacation.

We looked at Florida and North Carolina, but we decided to be adventuresome and go with a more exotic location, Bermuda.

A small, hilly island with lush, subtropical vegetation, Bermuda's coastal cliffs are interspersed with magnificent beaches and sheltered coves of pink sand.

Leafing through the piles of color brochures, I noted something else: that Bermuda was a mere speck in the North Atlantic, a tiny island with only one paved airport and who knew how many hospitals.

But this paradise was only a two-hour flight from New York, so Leo and I took the plunge.

When we stepped off the plane to balmy air and swaying palms, we were both ecstatic. After years of gray hospital rooms, we were like two kids playing hooky.

As soon as we checked into our hotel room, I hung my head out the window, admiring the long blue shoreline, the pastel houses dotting the horizon. Leo set about making reservations for every night of our weeklong visit—fresh fish on the waterfront, boat tours, fireworks on the beach.

For those first two days, we were in seventh heaven. Everything thrilled me: the sound of the surf audible from our bedroom, the pink sand, and orange sunsets. But on the third day, even as we shopped and relaxed, I could sense in the margins of my consciousness that something was wrong.

It began with chills that soon alternated with diarrhea and nausea, then waves of burning fever. I thought I might be able to sleep it off, but by the next morning I couldn't ignore the fact that I was definitely ill.

I was sure that I'd caught some kind of bug during the plane ride, a perfect petri dish for viruses. If it weren't for my compromised immune system, I wouldn't have worried. But when I checked with my transplant center and described my symptoms, the doctors sounded alarmed.

"It could be CMV," they told me, referring to cytomegalovirus, a common infection that is potentially fatal for someone like me. They urged me to return home immediately and check in with them. That seemed alarmist, but they had been the very people who had worked so hard to keep me alive. With a heavy heart, I eventually compromised by agreeing to return to the States and go to an emergency room.

As hard as this was for me, I felt worse for Leo. When I hung up and told him the verdict, I could see by his face how disappointed he was. But he tried valiantly not to show it, and opened the closet to begin packing our clothes.

Within an afternoon, we were shuttled from paradise back to the drab world of a New Jersey hospital, a venue where we were sadly accustomed.

Emergency rooms had been one of the main destinations of our young marriage. In fact, we'd been to so many that Leo had begun comparing their attributes and designs. This one was especially gloomy—windowless with a malfunctioning heater.

It didn't help that my body was still accustomed to tropical flowers and golden light. Now here we were, seated on broken plastic chairs, with ancient magazines and scuffed linoleum, surrounded by throngs of people who were equally ill.

I had been through this kind of health scare so many times that I was still convinced I only had a simple virus. Throughout our marriage, I'd told Leo, "I'll give you a hundred and one scares, but I'll always pull through."

After many hours of tests and intravenous antibiotics, I was finally released the next morning with oral antibiotics and a stern order from the doctor that if my temperature climbed again, I must immediately return to the hospital.

By the next day, my temperature had indeed spiked even higher, and we found ourselves in yet another emergency room, this one run by a particularly sour and impatient doctor with a thatch of blond hair and exhausted eyes.

"I've got an ER to run, what's your problem?" she asked when she entered my cubicle.

I gave her the condensed version of my body's history. She seemed annoyed at the complexity of my case and the time it required. Even as I talked, I could feel my body tense at her brusqueness. And when she pressed hard on my kidneys during her examination, I cried out in pain.

"Well, that's worrisome," she said, drawing back, and looking at me with a frown. "I'm going to have to call the transplant team." With that, she walked out, and the dark cloud she left in her wake settled over me.

I hadn't seriously considered that I might actually be in trouble until that moment. But her comment, drawn face, and the pain I'd felt under her hand all threw me into such a panic that I burst into tears.

What if my second kidney were failing?

Luckily, I was saved, as I have so often been, by the kindness of strangers. The ultrasound technician whom I was sent to next was a compassionate older woman who had worked at the hospital for many years.

Once she settled me onto her examining table, I saw that she had decorated the ceiling with butterflies and luminous planets in order to give patients a soothing distraction.

She applied a sound-conducting jelly to my abdomen, then passed a handheld instrument called a transducer over the skin where the jelly was applied. The transducer sent sound waves into my body, which bounced off my kidneys and echoed back to it. The echoes were then converted to images displayed on a screen.

Even though the technician was not supposed to report on what she saw, she took pity on me.

"You have beautiful kidneys. Take a look," she said, and pointed at the screen. There they were, like glowing kidney beans. This was the first time I'd ever viewed them, and I felt my heart soften at the sight—the way a pregnant woman must feel when she first views her baby.

The technician pointed out the blood flowing through each organ with what looked like golden light. Then she turned up the sound so I could actually hear the *pssh, pssh* of flowing blood. This was my great gift, my source of life, and they were healthy, just as I had originally intuited. I calmed down as I observed them, gleaming in my pelvis.

Later that evening, five days after we'd originally left on our trip, Leo and I were back home, finally unpacking the luggage from our unexpected saga.

Early in our vacation we'd bought a small watercolor by a local painter that perfectly depicted the view from our hotel window—the ocean and the sweet pastel houses on the horizon.

I took it out of our bags and studied it a moment. It was as if a window had been thrown open, bringing back the warm scent of those balmy nights. I placed the painting behind a mirror on my bureau. It was too painful; I didn't want either of us to dwell on it. I wanted to pretend this vacation had never happened. I didn't want to be reminded of how vulnerable I'd felt, of how much pleasure we'd forfeited.

In fact, Leo and I had already tacitly agreed that it was too risky for us to leave the country or travel so far again. Planes probably weren't a great idea—or ships either, for that matter. We would play it safe, stick near home. In the wake of our recent experience, we would whittle down the dimensions of our future to local venues. Deciding this made me feel prudent and practical, yet sad.

But as the days passed, I found myself sliding the painting out whenever I was alone in our bedroom. Those little purple flowers—were they bougainvillea? And what color would you call that sea—cerulean, azure? In spite of myself, I couldn't stop looking and remembering.

One morning as we were getting ready for work, Leo pulled out the painting and said, "Why don't we hang this up?"

I looked at him in surprise. "Okay. Where?"

He led me out to our central foyer through which we passed many times each day. "How about here?"

He got a hammer and nail, and I stood behind him as he carefully mounted the painting near our front door. We both stood studying it.

"Let's go back next year," I said after a moment.

Leo straightened the painting, then reached over and took my hand.

Sometimes courage can be as small as that—hanging a painting, saying the words "Next year," deciding to try again.

Twelve

LEARNING TO HUG

I went to a book expo where there was an appearance by Martin Neufeld, who had recently published *Hugging Life,* about the transformational aspects of this simple human expression.

Hugging, it turns out, is highly therapeutic for our physical and emotional well-being, stimulating among other things a deep relaxation response. Across cultures, hugging signifies affection and caring. In fact, it seems to be essential to our human natures, warming both our hearts and bodies.

But you wouldn't have known this from the reaction the author received at the expo.

In order to promote his book, he stood with his arms outstretched, a broad smile on his face, next to a sign that read: "Free Hugs."

I watched people rush by him, with defensive and guarded expressions. A few giggled, but most pointed or rolled their eyes. No one stepped up to be hugged by him.

I was waiting for a friend to meet me, and when she finally arrived, she noticed the hugger with his sign.

"Oh, this is great," she said, and walked promptly into the author's outstretched arms. He was thrilled that she'd stopped and taken him up on his offer. "You're the first person all day who's accepted," he told her.

We're accustomed to giving, but receiving makes us anxious, so we adopt a cynical, suspicious attitude, as if to protect ourselves.

Dr. Oliver Sacks, the author and neurologist, has been a popular speaker for our organization. One of his most compelling subjects is the professor and author Temple Grandin, who suffers from Asperger's-type autism. Because of her condition, Grandin can't tolerate human touch and has difficulty reading social cues. But being aware of the value of physical touch, especially hugging, she invented what she calls a squeeze machine, an industrial compressor of the type that fills tires with air. When she crawls into the machine and turns on the compressor, the squeeze machine exerts a firm pressure on her body that simulates a human hug.

In other words, she has devised an exquisitely modulated piece of equipment to simulate an act that the man at the book expo was unable to give away for free.

WHEN I WAS IN COLLEGE, I developed a major crush on a guy named Corey. In my teenage heart, I poured all my longing into him, endlessly daydreaming about what it would be like if we were together. And what did I imagine specifically? In various scenes and settings, I visualized myself enfolded in his embrace.

One day, I admitted my crush to a guy in my dorm named Mark, without realizing that he was a good friend of Corey's and frequently spoke to him.

The next day, Mark knocked on my dorm door and said matter-of-factly, "I told Corey you like him. He said you should wait for him after your history class tomorrow."

I was stupefied. "What? You told him?"

"Well, sure. You didn't tell me not to."

I was flushed with embarrassment. I couldn't believe how clueless guys could be. The part of me that was thrilled by the fact that Corey actually might be interested in me was flooded over with a dozen fears.

Would Corey think I had asked Mark to speak to him? Would he think I was pushy and pathetic? Then I spiraled down even further. Corey didn't really know me—would he be disappointed when we met? What would I say to him?

In my mind's eye, I had turned Corey into a paragon of perfection—handsome, funny, sexy. How could I possibly meet him, vulnerable and flawed as I was?

By the next day, I was so anxious that I skipped history class entirely—the possibility of actually meeting Corey had been transformed into a dreaded event. Instead, I sat in my dorm room and watched the clock move past the appointed hour, from ten to eleven, then twelve. I was depriving myself of a long-held fantasy, but I couldn't budge. I felt terrible on so many levels—sad and disappointed, mostly in myself. I hadn't realized until then how insecure I was.

Later I found out that Corey had waited half an hour for me, then left, thinking that I had changed my mind and wasn't interested after all. As far as I know, he never learned otherwise.

Because I didn't want to look foolish, because I didn't feel confident enough about myself to receive his attention, I lost out on meeting this young man and possibly the comfort of that long-imagined embrace.

THE PHYSICIAN AND AUTHOR Bernie Siegel talked to us recently about his personal transformation from a conventional doctor who kept his patients at arm's length to a more compassionate role. Western medical training had taught him to be the cool bestower of advice and wisdom while his patients were the passive recipients, mute and grateful. With the advent of specialization, managed care, and rigid time restraints, the bedside manner of the old-fashioned healing physician had vanished.

But Siegel realized the limitations of this paradigm, for patients and himself, and began to inch across the imaginary divide between doctor and patient. A gifted artist, he showed us a self-portrait painted during his early career in which he looked haggard and distraught. Then he showed us another self-portrait, done after he'd begun to interact with more compassion and intimacy. In this portrait, his face had softened; he had a warm smile and new inner glow.

What was the most profound thing that had changed his relations with his patients? He had begun hugging them, he told us.

Hugs may be just what we all need in our fractious, wary world. Chris Thompson, a *Saginaw News* columnist, writes: "Most of us have a little person inside who needs human contact in this stainless steel, computerized society where we are kept at arm's length."

The popularity of India's "hugging saint," Mata Amritanandamayi, known as Amma, bears this out. Thousands of people from all over the world wait in line for hours to receive a simple hug from her.

According to *USA Today*: "Her arms are open to all: infants and elderly, Christians and Jews, Hindus and Buddhists . . . anyone longing to be enveloped."

It is rare for a single woman from a traditional Hindu culture to bestow such an intimate personal blessing, let alone touch a stranger. Yet Amma, a tiny woman under five feet tall, has been known to hug twenty-thousand people in a single session and willingly embraces and consoles anyone who is in need.

Personally, I'm one of the world's biggest huggers—in fact, my husband, Leo, gets a weary look on his face when he sees that I'm preparing to wrap him up in another one. I snuggle my face into his neck and breathe in his unique scent. I can feel my body relax against his; I can hear the thump of his heart next to mine.

We humans need each other, and hugs—so powerful, so easy— remind us just how much.

Thirteen

THE BEST MEDICINE

After a particularly grueling day at the hospital following my first transplant, my mother and I often collapsed in front of the TV and watched reruns of *I Love Lucy*. By the light of the TV, I could see my mom's face soften as she laughed at these comedies. I didn't need research to appreciate the therapeutic effects of her laughter—I could almost see the endorphins being released as she chuckled and guffawed.

In fact, in dealing with my illness, my mother and I were a team that often resembled Lucy and Ethel, bumbling along, with mishaps at every turn. My mother was notoriously absentminded, she once left her car keys in the ignition and her car running at the curb at Newark airport as she rushed to board a plane with me to California. It wasn't until we were airborne, somewhere over Ohio, that she turned to me and said, "Oh, my God!" Luckily, we were able to locate the security guard at the airport who had moved the car and safely parked it. He had been waiting to hear from the lunatic who'd pulled such a stunt.

. . .

WHEN MY KIDNEYS began to fail, my mother and I read about the benefits of a macrobiotic diet and decided we should try it in an attempt to save my kidneys.

This diet was composed of grains, especially brown rice, along with vegetables, seeds, miso, and beans. It was extremely bland and rigid; you weren't allowed processed, sugared, or canned foods, and no fruits and vegetables that were not in season. All food was supposed to be cooked over a gas fire, since electricity—let alone microwaves—was said to cause chaotic energy patterns, whatever they were.

In the middle of South Jersey, these kinds of strictures were especially onerous. This diet couldn't have been more opposite from the fragrant pizzas and greasy burgers that my contemporaries were eating.

But in order to help save my kidneys, we were willing to try it. My mother's refrigerator soon resembled a miniature greenhouse, stuffed with what looked like foliage and weeds.

When I was hospitalized in Philadelphia, she often went out late at night, roaming the streets for a health food store. One evening, she breathlessly returned to plunk down in front of me several containers filled with funky-looking concoctions—slimy strands of roots and leaves.

"What's that?" a nurse asked with distaste when she uncovered a dish of what looked like long, pale carrots.

"It's daikon, actually, the Asian white radish—very healthy," my mother reported airily.

In loyalty to me, she defended this diet, and tried to act as if she were following it herself.

"Wow, isn't this good," she said as we both dipped into a bland kidney bean puree.

But at that moment, I could see a Reese's peanut butter cup, half gnawed, stashed in her purse.

EVEN THOUGH SHE was a terrible cook, she tried making several recipes. One day when I was headed out of the house, I saw her busily unpacking a bag of strange herbs.

"Don't look, I'm making surprise soup. It'll be waiting when you get back," she said.

But when I opened the door that evening, the house didn't smell like soup, but a florist's shop.

My mother was beaming. "It's been cooking for hours!"

I looked at the maroon-tinted brew in the soup pot.

"It's the kind of thing you have to get used to," she told me. "Just have a little."

She poured some into a bowl and placed it in front of me.

I took a small sip and immediately rushed to the sink to spit it out. "This is terrible! What is it?"

I looked at the package she'd thrown into the wastebasket. The label read: "rosebud and eucalyptus holiday potpourri."

"These aren't herbs, they're potpourri, to make the room smell good."

"Oh, God, what if I've poisoned you!" She pulled out the phone book and began rifling through it.

"What are you doing?"

"Calling the poison control center."

"I just had a little. I spit it out. Plus, I'm sure they don't have an antidote for rosebud soup."

I began to laugh and then she looked up and joined me in spite of herself. You had to laugh. We'd already learned that.

BESIDES MY MOTHER, I had another family member to keep me laughing: my maternal grandmother, a comedienne who could have come straight from the Borscht Belt. She was a real character, dramatic and unpredictable. She once left her pocketbook at the supermarket, but refused to claim it because inside were two apples she had stolen.

Although my grandmother regularly insisted that she was frail and near death, she was always out and about, dolled up in her costume-jewelry pearls and mangy fake mink. One time, when my mother and I were walking down Main Street in Allentown, we stopped as a parade approached.

"Ma, look," I cried, and there was my grandmother, not on death's door as she had asserted to us on the phone that morning, but perched on the opening float with the grand marshal, blowing kisses and waving.

After I became ill, her dramatics went into overdrive. When she called me in the hospital, I picked up the phone to hear her cry out, "Oh my God, you're so sick. Why oh why are you so sick!" and then hang up; no hello, no good-bye.

Luckily, rather than upsetting me, my grandmother always made me laugh.

WHEN I DIDN'T have my diet and my madcap relatives to keep my dark humor intact, there were my romances . . . or lack of them.

During my college years, when I went on dialysis, there was nothing funny about the process.

When your kidneys are healthy, they clean your blood and produce hormones that keep your bones strong. But when they fail, you need dialysis to replace the work they once performed. Dialysis filters the blood to rid your body of harmful wastes, extra salt, and water.

In order to receive this treatment, I had a catheter surgically attached to the peritoneal cavity of my abdomen. Five times each day, I had to wash my hands repeatedly, put on a medical mask, then sterilely connect my catheter to tubing which I hung on an IV pole in my bedroom. Then I had to wait while two liters of fluid drained from my stomach area.

This took a chunk out of the normal ebb and flow of my student day—I went to class, then rushed back home for treatment—and it put a real crimp in my romantic life.

Still, I went out to parties with my roommates whenever I could, determined to live as normally as possible.

One night at a party, I met a gorgeous Italian student and ended up at his apartment, draped across his bed, as he interpreted opera arias that were filling his bedroom with crescendos of sound.

I was in a dreamy fog—it was all so enchanting: this young man murmuring Italian, the cozy room, the rain that fell in the balmy night. The only thing interfering was the two-foot-long catheter that was taped securely to my stomach, a long plastic reminder of my medical condition. It felt huge and obvious.

So when, on romantic cue, the Italian's hands began roaming my body, I stiffened, unsure what part of my body I was most nervous about. I was shy about being flat-chested, so I definitely didn't want him touching my breasts; but I didn't want him to feel my cathetered abdomen, or roam lower either, for that matter.

I snuggled under the covers, pretending to be chilled. I tried to relax as the arias continued, but I saw by the illuminated clock that time was marching by, as much as I was trying to ignore it.

You can put off dialysis for a while, but once toxins begin to accumulate, you get a metallic taste in your mouth. I began to taste it, just as my Italian friend was nuzzling my neck.

The rain had grown fierce by then; we were in the middle of a serious thunderstorm.

"Why don't you stay over?" he asked, cuddling up to my swathed form.

I felt like Cinderella—I had to get out of there. There was no way I could undress in front of him, let alone stay the night.

So I had to face facts and let go of this balloon of a dream.

"Look, I have to tell you something," I started. "I have kidney failure and I'm on dialysis. I have to get home and have a treatment."

There's nothing to pierce a romantic bubble like the word "dialysis."

I almost felt sorry for him as I watched his face. Poor guy, he probably picked up girls all the time—the last thing he'd expected was a medical dilemma. In fact, of all the parts of my body he had hoped to learn about that night, I'm sure my kidneys weren't among them.

But he was a gentleman. "I still like you—I still want to see you," he insisted as he walked me out to my car.

Yeah, yeah. I thanked him, drove home, and hooked myself up to the machine, certain I'd never hear from him again. And I was right—I never did.

I'll admit it took a few years for me to fully appreciate the dark humor of that evening. But over time, I consoled myself that someone as fickle as he would have never worked out in the long run. Still, whenever I hear Pavarotti sing "Che gelida manina"—what a cold little hand—I think of that night when I briefly starred in a mini version of *La Bohème* in New Brunswick, New Jersey.

Oh, well. At least he never discovered how flat-chested I was.

Fourteen

WRITING YOUR LIFE

If you peeked into a certain second-floor window at a children's hospital in Philadelphia in 1989, you would have seen two women, one in her late teens, another in her sixties, bent over paper, writing—my mother and me.

I wrote diaries, journals, and letters throughout my illness, and my mother did the same.

We wrote to cope, to chronicle, to release our emotions and make sense of our pain.

We wrote while we waited on news and after we received it. Wherever we traveled, there were notebooks, scraps of paper, and journals all around us, covered with the chicken scratch of our fears and feelings. We kept a day-by-day account not just of the tests, procedures, doctors, and diagnoses, but also of our feelings. How scared we were, how confused and vulnerable.

It wasn't until later, when I read about the healthful benefits of writing, that I realized we were intuitively involved in a process that was deeply therapeutic.

Writing—and letters—formed the basis of my organization.

Before the days of e-mail, most of the people I matched in Friends' Health Connection didn't call each other on the telephone but communicated by the old-fashioned laying down of words.

Early on, two special people were brought together by my organization—a young midwestern woman in her twenties, who was suffering from a serious cancer, and another young woman in Alaska, who was afflicted with a rare immune disease. I couldn't find anyone who was suffering from the exact same disorder as the Alaskan patient, but I was struck by how similar the letters of these two women were—their isolation and yearning for companionship. I thought they would relate to each other, and they did.

They wrote each other every week, revealing their fears and feelings. "How glad I am to find you. I feel I know you even though we've never met; you understand just how I feel." They discovered how powerful and affirming it was to write down their deepest emotions and share them with someone who cares and understands.

They had been writing each other for several years, when Oprah Winfrey arranged for a surprise meeting on a show she was airing about friendship and support.

I was in on the planning of this reunion, but watched it on television from home. Oprah walked over to the cancer patient, who was frail and pale, and asked her to talk about her pen pal.

"Do you think you'll ever meet your friend in person?" Oprah asked when she was finished.

"I don't know—but I hope so," the woman responded.

Oprah said, "Well, how about now . . . turn around."

When the woman turned around, her FHC friend was sitting right behind her (she had been let in on the surprise).

What I remember most about that show was the two women meeting each other's eyes—the way their faces changed and brightened with recognition and pleasure as they held on to each other and cried. I thought how that deep bond—one that lasted until the cancer patient died shortly after the taping—had been forged by words.

There is something in the nature of writing about our thoughts and feelings that is cathartic and healing. In her book *Listen to Me: Writing Life into Meaning,* Lynn Lauber writes: "There is a potency to the act of writing words that sets it apart from simply speaking them, a process that seems to take place between the brain and the pen."

Research suggests that writing about emotional experiences can result in tangible benefits in health. According to Dr. James Pennebaker, a pioneer in the use of expressive writing for healing, "When people are given the opportunity to write about emotional upheavals, they often experience improved health. They go to the doctor less. They have changes in immune function."

Well-known authors such as Joan Didion have used the power of writing to process grief and loss. Didion says that she wrote her memoir, *The Year of Magical Thinking,* as a road back to sanity after the sudden death of her novelist husband and their only daughter.

It's not that writing makes pain or loss go away, but there is something about translating an experience into a coherent narrative that can make it more graspable. It can put our experiences into context and make us view our lives—and selves—in a new way. And the best thing is that this kind of writing is available to anyone. No training, no special talent is necessary.

Writing can also provide a crucial link to history, a way of keeping the past alive: In her book *Writing Alone and with Others,* Pat Schneider makes a suggestion: imagine going back to the house where your great-great-grandmother once lived and finding only a stone foundation, then moving a stone to find a small sheaf of paper.

"On those pages your great-great-grandmother has written in tiny letters. It isn't fancy writing. She's writing what your grandfather said when he came in to tell her that the potatoes had all rotted. She's writing about her baby that just died."

She asks us to imagine these words, then asks: "Wouldn't that be a treasure?"

This happened in real life to Ann Kirschner, but with her mother, Sala, as she chronicles in her book *Sala's Gift.* As a young Jewish girl growing up during World War II, for Sala writing was a means of survival, but it was a reality she kept secret for fifty years. She arrived in America as a war bride and raised a family without speaking to any of them about her experiences during the war. It was only on the eve of a scheduled heart surgery that she finally showed her daughter more than 350 letters, along with a diary that she had kept hidden in a cardboard box. These letters documented the five years she had spent as a slave in seven separate Nazi labor camps.

Her chronicle of life as a seamstress and laundress for the Germans provides a rare peek into the world of labor camps, where captured Jews were forced, under brutal conditions, to build munitions and highways that helped sustain the German war effort.

Unlike Auschwitz, where Sala lost most of her family, labor camps allowed inmates to receive and send letters. The expressions of support and love in these letters, which Sala saved at great personal risk, helped her endure her exile and suffering.

In one letter, Sala's friend Rauzek writes to her in May 1942: "Be happy, be glad, and thank God a thousand times every day that you still have somebody to whom you can write with the way things are going here. . . ."

Oliver Sacks has written that "we need stories that normalize our suffering and show us we are part of a community of pain, sin and suffering. We need to be known, to be understood."

Sala's letters are a reminder of all writing can do—not only provide a lifeline and support in the midst of a hell like Sala's, but also educate and inspire those in the future who are lucky enough to read them.

Fifteen

MODELS OF INSPIRATION

The Central Park Jogger spoke for our organization one evening. That's how I—and most people—still thought of her, even after she released her identity to the public. Trisha Meili was such a symbol of hope that a mere name didn't seem to contain her.

Petite and stylish, with a cap of frosted hair, she walked confidently to the podium. A small scar near her eye was the only visible sign of what she had endured over a decade before.

In April 1989, when she was twenty-eight, Meili had been attacked and raped while jogging in Central Park, suffering two skull fractures and losing at least three-fourths of her blood. She was beaten so severely that she was barely recognizable, even to her family and friends. In the end, she was identified by a small gold ring that her parents had given her.

After being administered last rites, Meili spent two weeks in a coma. Doctors said if she lived she would likely be severely brain damaged; one doctor commented that it might be better if she died.

As she fought to recover from her massive injuries, the senselessness of the crime captured the imagination of people all over the world.

The New York hospital where she was being cared for was besieged by strangers offering help. Blood donations, prayers, and flowers poured in from all over the country, including a dozen roses from Frank Sinatra.

When she emerged from the coma, Meili could no longer remember details of the attack but she had to face long months of prolonged and arduous recovery—learning how to talk, feed herself, think abstractly, and walk.

Her healing continued for well over a decade. Fourteen years after the attack, in an autobiography, she broke her silence to discuss the incident in her own words and reveal who she was before the attack and how it changed her life.

In her talk, Meili reminded us that the body is not a machine that can be swiftly repaired after a trauma. While our measure of successful healing is to return to the selves we were before, she has had to accept that she will never be the same. But Meili has learned to be proud of how far she's advanced rather than regret the distance she has to travel.

What amazed our audience was the lack of rancor that Meili held toward the young men who'd attacked her, how she focused on her recovery, the lessons she'd learned, and those who had helped her along the way.

Someone in the audience asked: "But how can you not be furious?"

"I can't waste my time being angry," she replied. "I have to move forward. I focus on the positives. And I realize I've seen both the best and worst of humanity."

Meili has used her own recovery to help others, by speaking at rehab hospitals to both clinicians and head-injury patients.

Referring to a recent speech, she said: "At the end of my talk, a gentleman in a wheelchair raised his hand and said, 'I was in a coma for three and a half months, and the doctors didn't think I was ever going to walk again—but seeing you has been so inspiring. Were you ever in a wheelchair?' I said yes. Then he said, 'I'm going to get out of this wheelchair.' That made me feel so good."

I noticed several people in our audience who were in wheelchairs, their faces tilted up, transfixed as they soaked up her encouraging words.

We all need role models to inspire and guide us. Other people's lives matter deeply to us and can shape how we approach our own trials.

Trisha Meili could have licked her wounds and chosen to remain anonymous. But instead she found her voice and put it in the pubic domain, along with her name and photograph. She shared the most personal account of her struggle to learn to walk and talk again. She would not be brought down—either by her attackers or by those who criticized her for jogging alone.

This woman lives her special destiny and leaves a trail that others could follow.

AS I WAS READING *The New York Times* one afternoon, I was reminded of another woman of great strength and courage who I'd known of when I was young, then put out of my mind.

Growing up in Atlantic City, she was a familiar sight on the boardwalk—a quadriplegic street musician who lay on her stomach on a gurney and played an electric synthesizer with her tongue. At thirteen, I'd never witnessed anyone so disabled. She was an astounding sight, like a dusky mermaid who'd been swept up onto the boardwalk. She usually stationed herself in front of Caesars Palace. There the stupefied public gathered as she played "Somewhere Over the Rainbow" and "America the Beautiful," and then dropped cash in a can by her side.

So many offbeat characters populated Atlantic City that I soon became accustomed to the sight of her moving along the boardwalk on the motorized gurney that she guided with a steering device worked by her chin.

At that point, I was embarking on what I assumed would be a carefree teenage life. At thirteen, I had lied about my age in order to get a fast-food job that had landed me in the center of beach life. My workstation overlooked the vast and tumbling Atlantic. Lifeguards, bronzed and handsome, wandered in to flirt and order sandwiches and sodas. I came home each evening drenched in sun, the scent of salt in my hair. I had every reason to believe that the rest of my life would be a variation on this breezy theme.

So I hurried by the piano lady on my way to work, regarding her with the pity I felt for anyone severely disabled. But I never dawdled or spoke to her. She really had nothing to do with me; hers was a reality as distant to mine as someone from another planet. And with the sweep of my own life, I forgot about her.

Until I opened the newspaper one day and read an obituary headline in *The New York Times:* Celestine Tate Harrington, 42, quadriplegic street musician, "whose buoyant personality and unremitting chutzpah brought astounded smiles to everyone who watched her play the keyboard with her lips and tongue on Atlantic City's Boardwalk."

What I hadn't known about this woman—what we don't know about the hidden bravery of most people's lives—could have filled a book.

According to the obituary, although Harrington suffered from a congenital joint condition that had rendered her legs and arms useless, she had never considered herself disabled. Her mother had tried to abort her, and she had been abandoned by her father when she was a child. Harrington had been raised by her grandparents, and later had a child of her own. She won the right to keep custody of her child after she displayed to an amazed judge how she was able to change her baby's diapers with her teeth.

She learned to play the keyboard at Philadelphia's Settlement Music School, arriving on the boardwalk in 1984. She eventually moved into an Atlantic City condo that she purchased with proceeds from her entertaining and became known for the inspiring message of fortitude that she spread on talk shows and to those she met. One of these was Camille LeClair, co-owner of a McDonald's where Harrington once worked taking phone orders.

LeClair was quoted in the obituary about an occasion when Harrington was visiting her house. "I hopped in the shower and when I came back I said to Celestine, 'Why does God allow me to jump in and out of the shower in ten minutes, but you have to struggle so much?' Well, Celestine just looked at me and said, 'That's why I'm here. To keep reminding you to count your blessings every day.' "

That's what models of inspiration do—they lodge in us and

provide a compass, even when we don't consciously remember them. I had registered Celestine Harrington deep in my psyche, and reading about her death that day made her roll back into my mind.

It turned out that she had plenty to do with me, after all. By the time I saw her death notice, I'd had my own experience of physical suffering. I could finally appreciate the strength and grandeur that kept her making music on the boardwalk of Atlantic City—an apparition in a pink nightgown, a smile on her remarkable face.

Unlike Trisha Meili, she may have never written a book, but because you've read this, she's now alive in you, too.

Sixteen

ART THERAPY

As far as I was concerned, my mother was an artist wherever she was, but she combined her skills as a registered nurse and an artist and she earned a degree in art therapy.

During her professional life she often held jobs as an art therapist in hospitals and psychiatric settings, working with a range of patients from the very old to the very young.

When she came home in the evenings, she showed me drawings and paintings that patients had produced throughout the day, unrolling them on the floor so I could study them.

"What do you see in these?" she asked me. "Do they give you any feelings about this person?"

Often they did, even though they were usually rudimentary, of frenzied shapes and patterns. Occasionally I would see a face in them or a figure like a horse. Other times I would sense anger in a slash of color or sadness in a small, cramped landscape.

My mother told me that my interpretations were often right on target—that, indeed, the painter was depressed or isolated or frightened. This exercise taught me to pay attention to the components of a painting and the feelings they elicit.

One of the most common drawings was of a house, and there were many clues to glean from these. Sad, isolated people often drew a blank front without windows or doors for entry. A chimney, especially one with smoke coming from it, symbolized someone with an interior life. A path with a flowering border suggested a warm and welcoming presence.

Sometimes my family drew pictures and asked my mother to interpret them. My happily married aunt drew a house with two large front windows that seemed endless and continued right off the page. My mother said that this symbolized the vast love between my aunt and uncle. A cousin drew two stick figures, the female leaning in while the male stood erect and upright, indicating an unequal relationship. When I drew a tree with circles adorning the branches, my mother said this suggested creative development.

Although I viewed this as fun, I knew it could also be serious business. Once when my mother was working in a psychiatric hospital, a patient drew such a disturbing drawing that she showed it to her director. He took one look and went running toward the patient's room. But it was too late; the patient had already committed suicide.

I managed to develop my mother's love for art without inheriting her talent for drawing or painting, but her influence helped me appreciate the pleasure of crafts. I make pottery on the potter's wheel, knit and crochet, as well as one of my most favorite activities, making tile mosaics. I take old dishes bought at yard sales and smash them to bits with a hammer—which is therapeutic in itself.

Then I use these colorful bits to re-create a new and beautiful pattern. My house is full of these creations, as well as artwork my mother left after her death.

Most precious to me are her oil paintings, several that include the two of us. In fact, right after she died, I took many of them to my office so they could hang near me. I loved it when people stopped and studied them and asked me questions. It was as if a part of her were still alive.

Only a few months after her death, while I was still deep in mourning, I walked into work one morning and found that the office had been vandalized.

Desks were turned over, filing cabinets were on their sides, paper strewn everywhere. There was a new scent in the room, hot and electric. Later, I discovered that nothing had been stolen, but I was unable to concentrate on that part of my luck.

The worst thing the vandals had done was deface my mother's paintings. One of my favorites, a large oil painting of her holding me when I was a baby, had vile words sprayed over our faces. Another, a portrait of me as a young woman, was splattered and slashed with black paint.

I couldn't believe how cruelly personal this felt, especially since I'd just recently lost her.

I called the police and reported the crime, but I couldn't face cleaning up the office. I went back home and crawled into bed and curled up in fetal position. I felt sad, violated, and angry, all of this overlaid by a thick layer of grief.

It took less than a week before the police found the culprits. An officer called me at work and asked if I wanted to press charges.

"Who were they?"

"Some local kids," he told me. "We caught them just as they were getting ready to break into another office. One's twelve and his brother's thirteen. They're well known in the courts because their folks are in jail all the time. The kids have been in and out of foster care all their lives. When we picked them up and asked who we should call, they said there was no one."

As the policeman talked, I was studying the painting of me in my mother's arms that was propped up against the wall. I was planning to take it to a museum restorer. I didn't have much hope that the painting could be fixed, but I was willing to spend any amount to try.

But instead of focusing on my loss, on the horrible way this crime had made me feel, something else started to happen.

Over the policeman's words, my mother's voice floated back to me, asking me the question she'd posed so many times in the past: *"What do you see in this painting, Roxanne? What do you see?"*

When he finished talking, I said to the policeman, "I don't want to press charges."

"Are you sure?"

I told him I was.

After I hung up, I sat looking at the painting. Instead of my own hurt, I saw the young vandals' deprivation—growing up on the streets, without parental love or attention, with no one to turn to or call. It was hard for me to imagine how this must feel, but I sat for a long time and tried.

"Okay, Ma, I see it," I whispered finally.

So this was art therapy, after all.

Seventeen

UNEXPECTED BLESSINGS

There's no denying the pain and trauma that accompany chronic illness, but confronting these challenges can often provide unexpected blessings, and one of them is the ability to truly savor the gift of life.

Alan Alda recently spoke to our organization about how he had been changed by a near-death experience.

In 2003, while on a remote mountaintop in Chile, he developed a nearly fatal intestinal obstruction. After being saved by emergency surgery, he found himself reexamining his life, anxious to find a way to get the most out of his renewed time. What makes a life meaningful? he asked himself, and he came up with several answers: staying receptive to new ideas and people, enjoying the journey as much as the destination, and being aware of everything around him.

Alda said he now tries to live in the present moment—meaning within the current five seconds—what scientists consider the *now*.

Anything before that is considered a memory and anything after that is considered the future, so now is constantly moving.

This kind of introspective shake-up is common among people who have faced life-and-death situations.

Lance Armstrong speaks of his cancer diagnosis as "the day it all changed. The day I started never to take anything for granted. The day I learned to take charge of my life."

In her book *Here's the Bright Side,* Betty Rollins, a two-time breast cancer survivor, writes about her surprising discoveries in the midst of her own illness: "People more than survive bum raps: they often thrive on them; they wind up stronger, livelier, and happier; they wake up to new insights and new people; and do better with the people around them who are not new." Experts, she reports, find that trauma doesn't just produce stress, but something termed "post-traumatic growth."

Years ago, when I was working on a publicity event for Andrew Weil in Chicago, we visited one of the coziest bookstores I'd ever entered. There were warm cherry bookshelves, comfy reading chairs, the scent of fresh brewed coffee in the air. The story behind the owners, a charming woman and her former banker husband, however, was what was really fascinating.

On a weekend trip to New York City, the couple had visited a tiny recovery bookstore that carried a variety of spiritual titles along with twelve-step material. Both had long been disillusioned with their stressful jobs and were each involved in recovery programs of their own to deal with their harried lives. As they left, they joked about opening such a store themselves someday.

A week later, on a weekend trip through Wisconsin, a drunk

driver crossed four lanes of highway traffic, careened out of control, and hit them head-on, demolishing their car. Watching the paramedics wheel his wife into an ambulance, the husband vowed to give up his commodity trading job and open the bookstore. After his wife was released from the emergency room, they headed back to Chicago, battered and bruised, and set about making their new enterprise a reality.

The bookstore was such a success with locals that they soon had to expand. Years later, their bustling bookstore was the result, featuring a lecture series hosting authors, a paid book club, and a Buddhist reading group.

After I heard their story, I understood the warm aura I felt when I entered the store. This couple's someday had come upon them suddenly, with a jolt, after their terrible accident. Trauma and illness often do that—they make you realize that tomorrow is no longer good enough.

When I stayed in Pittsburgh after my first transplant, at twenty-one, I met another girl, a little younger than I was, named Laura, who had just had a heart-lung transplant.

Laura was like the beautiful dolls I always wanted for Hanukkah—blond-haired, with a rosy complexion, porcelain skin, and a radiant smile. Before her transplant, she'd been so gravely ill that she'd been unable to walk across a room without turning blue from lack of oxygen. The doctors had told her that if she didn't get a heart and lung soon she wouldn't survive. It had been a long, tense wait for Laura and her family.

Then one day while she was in church, her beeper went off and she was notified that a compatible heart and lung had come in and she had to travel to Pittsburgh immediately for transplantation.

I met Laura when we both were recovering from our surgeries. She was so delighted to be able to walk that she convinced me to shun the elevator and enjoy something I'd never really appreciated before, the pleasure of climbing stairs. During those weeks, I followed her long legs and blond braid up many stairs. Her energy and optimism were an infectious energizer.

In the evening, Laura and I talked for hours. She was full of elaborate plans for all that she would be able to do now that she had a healthy body. "What I want most is to have a baby when I'm older," she told me. "I want to carry it in my body. I dream of that."

Laura eventually received permission to leave Pittsburgh and return home. Soon afterward, I got my discharge as well.

"We'll always keep in touch, let's promise," she said, and I vowed that we would.

I added Laura to my mailing list at work so that she received my newsletters and we upheld our promise to keep in touch. I heard about her family and her school life. But caught in the upsweep of my own world, perhaps it wasn't enough.

One day, about three years after our transplants, a letter I had sent to her was returned to me with the word "Deceased" stamped on it. Deceased? Laura? It seemed impossible that two such words could be linked together. But there they were.

I still think of the life force in Laura and the future she thought she had. She is a reminder for me not to dwell in the elusive future, but to appreciate the present moment—all we really have.

. . .

IN MY OWN CASE, I can vouch for a new sweetness to life after my lupus diagnosis. Unless you've had your health threatened, it's hard to imagine the sheer miracle of the most mundane of bodily functions—the way your head swivels on your neck or your feet flex at the end of your legs.

Even something as ordinary as urination has come to mean something profound. For so long, I had to hook up to tubing and machines in order to cleanse my body of toxins. Now each time I go to the bathroom, that little shower of liquid is like music.

There were so many years when I lived in chronic pain that to wake up without it is the most profound gift.

And my hair! Who would think my brunette tresses would mean so much, but they do. Once I'd lost most of mine due to medications. I remember going for a haircut and the stylist telling me dismissively, "Come back when you have enough hair to cut," and the sting I felt at her comment.

Now the simple fact that I have sufficient hair to walk into any salon without notice is something I actively savor.

This is not to say I don't have limitations; I do. But I've found ways to adapt and live around them.

As an outdoor person, one of the most difficult limitations is that I am no longer able to go out into the sun because ultraviolet rays can trigger lupus. So I've learned to delight in that small window of time when the sun is just beginning to set—that golden hour when the shadows are long.

That's my hour, the time I can go in the ocean for a quick swim or take a walk, and live my limited outdoor existence.

My husband accompanies me on my swims to make sure I don't go out too far. When I'm out in the waves and look up at the vast, domed sky, I feel more thankfulness and peace than I ever experienced before I fell ill.

No one wants to be sick or injured. But at some point in life, these crises happen to all of us.

The challenge is to discover the blessing buried in adversity, the little jewel embedded in the rock.

Eighteen

GIVING CARE

The night I received the phone call for my second transplant, Leo and I had spent another long day in the emergency room. I had been on dialysis for some time and had been experiencing chest pain and anxiety.

That night when we arrived home from the emergency room, Leo was exhausted, having spent the day with me as I was tested and scanned.

"I'm going to bed early," he said. Just as he was dragging himself up the stairs, the phone rang.

Our caller ID displayed a number with a 412 area code, which meant it was Pittsburgh, which meant it was the transplant center. I grabbed up the receiver and heard the words we'd been waiting for: "We have kidneys for you."

This was the best possible news in the world for me, but there was also a catch.

They were two baby kidneys from an eight-month-old and therefore very tiny, which is why I was being offered the pair instead of just one. This presented real risks, especially during the critical two-day postsurgical period, when there would be a high chance of blood clotting because of the tiny young blood vessels in the baby organs.

Choosing the right kidney is crucial. Each time you have a transplant, it becomes more difficult to repeat the procedure, because your body builds up antibodies.

"You can take or decline them, but you have to make the decision right away," the transplant center told me, as if the kidneys were a precious sales item that was going fast, which in fact was true.

But how was I supposed to decide?

Leo, now in his pajamas, sat at the top of the stairs, listening as I called the dialysis nurse and then the transplant surgeon, debating the pros and cons.

Finally the transplant surgeon said something that helped me: "If you were my daughter, I'd say to take them."

In the end it was possible that these young organs could last longer than an older kidney. So I decided to accept this gift.

The transplant team told us that we had to drive rather than fly to Pittsburgh immediately and that I shouldn't do any of the driving myself. So my weary husband packed us, and we left our house at midnight for the six-hour car ride.

Once at the hospital, we were caught up in a whirlwind of activity. I think I was less nervous than Leo. I'd been through this before, but he was going to be relegated to the most helpless of positions—sitting with strangers for hours in the waiting area, imagining what was happening in an operating room floors away.

As I was wheeled away on the stretcher, I watched his worried face recede into the distance.

"I'll be okay," I told him, and luckily I was; the operation was a success.

After the transplant, I was released after only two days to a family house filled with other transplant recipients and their care-givers, as well as those waiting for a transplant. The house was designed for those who weren't sick enough to be in the hospital but not healthy or strong enough to return home.

This communal world was even more of a shock for Leo. We were in the midst of a population of ill people, often hairless, pulling IVs up and down the halls.

A wife from Indiana was taking care of her husband as he waited for a double-lung transplant. She ate dinner with us many evenings and sat with us afterward, sharing photos of her grandkids. One day we found out that my new kidneys were functioning well, and were eager to share our good news with her. But as soon as she sat down with us that evening, her face collapsed and she began crying. Her husband had just died.

Leo had never been so close to such life-and-death dramas, to this parallel world where people were literally waiting for their lives.

Once I was released from the family house, I was as helpless as a rag doll. I couldn't sit up by myself, and even moving my head a few inches was painful. Leo had to carry me to the bathroom, feed me, even change my bedpan.

My immune system was so compromised that I had to remain homebound and isolated for three months to protect myself against germs. This meant no social life or visitors. Sometimes people left casseroles at the front door, as if for a leper, but otherwise no one could even come in to help us.

This is caregiving: grueling, relentless, emotionally and physically draining, even when it's performed out of great love.

THERE IS AN ART to being a patient just as there is to being a caregiver. If I had to choose, I think I'd rather be the patient than the other way around.

My mother was in her fifties and sixties when I became ill, and I became her project. My sisters were both grown and gone by then; she and my father were long separated, so she devoted herself to me.

I didn't shop, make my own meals, or even do my own laundry. Because I was ill, she picked up after me as if she were my personal handmaiden. Whenever I was hospitalized, she drove for hours to gather my mail and deliver it to my room.

This was all at the expense of her own serious health problems. Her asthma was severe by then, and growing worse, although she tried to hide it.

When I was in the hospital, she would occasionally disappear for extended periods, then return looking refreshed.

"Where've you been?"

"Oh, the gift shop."

Later I discovered that she'd gone to the pulmonary unit for oxygen because she was having such difficulty breathing.

When I received a scholarship to Rutgers University, I experienced my first taste of real independence, and my mother was delighted for me. This was what we had both always wanted—but it still hurt me to leave her alone.

"Don't worry about me, I'll be fine," she insisted.

But the day I moved out of our Atlantic City house into a dorm room, I returned to pick up some books and caught a glimpse of her through the window, crying on the stairs.

"I was just slicing onions," she said, when I rushed to her side. But that was such a flagrant lie—my mother was a terrible, infrequent cook—that it made me laugh before we both started crying again.

At college I shared a dorm room with three roommates who were compassionate without coddling me. When my health began deteriorating, they helped me out when I wasn't able to lift anything or drive. But they still included me on the chore schedule. I was expected to wash dishes and dust and help wherever I could.

This was crucial for me. I realized I was capable. I wasn't an invalid, as I'd so often felt with my mother.

DANA REEVE spoke for Friends' Health Connection about becoming a caregiver overnight after her husband, Christopher, was paralyzed from the neck down as a result of a horse riding accident.

Her world changed from the glamour of celebrity and limelight to the cold reality of breathing tubes and suppositories.

She spoke candidly about how essential she felt it was to maintain her role as a wife, separate from a caregiver, and how she rejected the label of hero, much as her husband did.

"When Chris and I got married," she said, "I took my wedding vows very seriously. . . . That was the day when I said, 'Okay, here we go. We're going on this journey, and let's hope it's a fun one.' Really, it has been."

Still, after her death, I couldn't help wondering whether the strain of her long support of her husband, and the emotional devastation of losing him, hadn't contributed to her own tragic death, two years later, from lung cancer.

AFTER MY SISTER BONNIE donated her kidney for my first transplant during my senior year in college, I became more independent than ever. And I wanted to show my mother how strong I was becoming.

I began building myself up and taking aerobics. I brought her to the gym to watch me work out and lift weights.

Ironically, as I was becoming stronger, she was growing weaker. I think some part of her was waiting to see that I was really well before she left me for good. It wasn't long after my transplant that she died.

If you take a good look around, you'll notice caregivers everywhere. They're the ones driving behind the ambulance, standing outside the emergency room, eating a takeout sandwich while picking up medication at a pharmacy drive-through. They have no nurses or helpers, but are left to fend for themselves.

In this age of extended life spans, we're likely to be not only our brother's keepers, but our friend's and neighbor's too.

It's important to acknowledge the great service involved in this, one of life's most blessed and challenging roles.

Nineteen

RANDOM ACTS OF KINDNESS

What do you do when no one is watching?

I remember a scene at the White House in 1992, after I had been appointed the 268th Daily Point of Light by President George H. W. Bush, an honor given to those who provide service to others. A total of a thousand Points of Light were honored by the president during his term.

We had just wandered through the First Lady's gardens and were out on the White House lawn, crowded with people from all over the country who were being similarly honored.

As spokesperson for the Youth Points of Light, I had already interviewed a number of the young people in attendance. One, a delicate blind girl named Stephanie, was a favorite. She visited schools around the country, acting out stories from Braille and familiarizing students with issues related to the blind. Her waiflike appearance belied her strength and determination.

Before lunch, we all gathered for a photo session. As small as Stephanie was, she became lost in the hubbub and ended up invisible from the camera, far in the back of the crowd. She was probably unaware of her position, but First Lady Barbara Bush noticed. She discreetly wove to the back and led Stephanie up front by the hand so that everyone could see her.

In the crush of the crowd, no one else seemed to register this small tender act, but I did. It was the kind of random kindness that I have so often been the beneficiary of myself.

AFTER *USA TODAY* did a cover story about me and Friends' Health Connection in 1992, I couldn't believe the response I received. I was bombarded with letters from all over the country. Amid the authentic requests from people interested in being matched, there were prison inmates proposing to marry me and shady operators offering get-rich-quick schemes.

So I was dubious when I received a call one day from a man who said he believed in what I was doing and wanted to help.

"Do you mind if I ask how you're paying yourself?" he said to me.

"Actually, I'm not," I told him.

I had received two grants from local sources—both amazing acts of generosity in themselves. The first, when I was only sixteen, came from a man named Dr. Irving Packer, who headed a foundation that funded worthy projects.

After him, there was Curt Weeden, then vice president of contributions at Johnson & Johnson, who heard about my work and not only provided me funding, but also took me under his wing, offering his expertise and advice. Neither he nor anyone in his company ever let me call the newspapers to thank or recognize Johnson & Johnson. I often read negative things about large companies without any mention of the positive—people like Curt Weeden, who was motivated to help me not out of profit or competition but sheer compassion.

These much-needed funds were used to finance my organization. But at the time of the stranger's call, I was receiving no salary and was, in fact, in quite a precarious position. When I'd graduated from college, I'd asked my mother if she would help support me for a year while I tried to make the organization thrive. At the time of the man's call, she was juggling several jobs to keep me and my vision afloat.

Then the phone rang, and this stranger materialized, saying he wanted to help.

When I opened the first envelope he sent me, I stared at the blue slip of paper inside, certain that it had to be a mistake—maybe the check was really for $350 or $3,500. I kept counting zeros. No, it was actually $35,000 that this man had donated to me and my life's work.

In the next decade he donated $50,000 a year without publicity or any desire for public acknowledgment. Without the support of him and his wife, the organization probably would not have survived.

In everyday life, people often perform these kind acts naturally without giving them a thought.

My friend Sam used to put change in other people's parking meters if he saw they were expired; my mother often paid the toll for the person behind her.

Another friend told me that each Halloween he hands out a huge deluxe chocolate bar, at more than two dollars apiece, to every child who knocks at his door.

"You must spend hundreds of dollars every Halloween," I told him.

He conceded that he did. "But it's worth it for the look of surprise on the kids' faces."

Organ donation may be the ultimate act of random kindness. Whenever you sign a donor card, you are in effect giving the gift of life to someone you will never know.

When I was staying in the family house in Pittsburgh after my last transplant, I became friendly with a close-knit Italian family, the Vitales, whose twenty-year-old son was waiting for a lung. If you need a kidney, you can at least survive for an extended period on dialysis. But for other organs—such as hearts, lungs, and livers—you have a limited time unless an organ can be found.

The Vitales, who had arrived at the home so hopeful, gradually grew more subdued and solemn as the days ticked by.

It is a terrible sadness to know that the life of your loved one is ticking away, that he could be saved with a donated organ, and that you're helpless to intervene. You can't save up to buy a heart or lung. You can't donate your own. There is nothing you can do but wait and pray.

Unlike other illnesses where there is no cure, doctors know exactly what is needed for transplants. They have the skills and know-how to keep a patient alive. All that's lacking is supply.

Soon it had reached the twenty-four-hour mark for the Vitales—their son had one more day to live without a new lung. I remember Mrs. Vitale as she sat over her breakfast that morning, trying to eat a bowl of cereal. In a month, her once round and rosy face had deflated, as if all the air and life had been drained from it.

That morning was the last time I saw her. The family was gone by the next day. Their son never received a new lung.

You hear about organ donations on television and read about them in brochures, but if anyone had sat with Mrs. Vitale that morning, they would gladly sign a donor card.

As a recipient myself of this ultimate gift, I find the words of donors' loved ones especially touching.

One mother of a tissue donor wrote on an Internet site about the death of her high schooler in a car accident after she fell asleep at the wheel following an evening of late-night reading.

Donating her daughter's eyes and heart was particularly symbolic to this mother—but because she also donated tissue, the impact of her daughter's gift was especially far-reaching. A dozen spinal surgeries were performed with the girl's donated bone, a man was healed from burns with her skin, two old women were able to walk again with her bone in their broken legs, a young woman recovered from brain tumor removal with her fascia.

The mother wrote: "I am profoundly grateful to know that my child—whose bones I knit, whose tissue I grew—lives on! Not only in spirit as I, and she, have always believed, but also in physical presence. Her gift literally embraces the world, an image that gives such comfort to us who love her."

And who is this woman? I tried to find her name, so I could quote her, but not surprisingly, she had chosen to remain anonymous, except for an Internet user ID.

YOU CAN LOOK AT random acts of kindness from a number of perspectives.

Buddhists believe they increase your karma and improve your future lives; Christians that they will help you reach heaven; in Judaism, mitzvot are good deeds performed out of commitment to the Jewish people.

But I like to think of it more simply: that there is a reservoir of goodwill out in the world, and each time you give you are replenishing it.

Twenty

SCAR TISSUE

In the drugstore the other day I saw a jar of scar-reduction cream that promised to flatten, soften, smooth, and blend scars with surrounding healthy skin.

If I wanted to get rid of the scars on my body, I'd need to buy at least a gallon of this stuff. However, I don't even want to get rid of my scars anymore. I consider them badges of survival.

But I didn't always feel this way.

As a teenager, I had stretch marks all over my body from weight fluctuations caused by steroid medication and kidney issues. My legs looked the worst, striped as a zebra's, so I began wearing panty hose at all times, even during the summer. But these stockings made me feel encased and trapped, like a walking sausage.

And people always noticed and asked me: "Why are you wearing panty hose with shorts?"

Next, I tried leg makeup, a thick camouflaging paste, but that also caused problems. It melted during the summer, leaving big splotches of color on my clothes or wherever I sat.

Then there was my face: it was so puffy from steroids that I decided to try a "miracle" face-lift. At $8.99, it wasn't much of a miracle—just two strips of adhesive tape that you placed behind your ears to pull your loose facial skin up and back. The problem was that whenever the wind blew, the tape was visible; also, if one side loosened, my face would become lopsided, like a cake taken out of the oven too soon.

These pathetic attempts were in addition to the regular regime of camouflage and concealment that was part of being young, self-conscious, and never happy with my body.

I always wore padded bras, tucked in my behind, and sucked in my stomach when I was out in public. During romantic encounters, I made sure I wore long pants and that the lights were turned down low.

As much effort as these machinations took, they were sadly ineffective; I never hid much of anything.

This was all before I knew what a real scar was—the kind that results from a kidney transplant. There is no hiding this scar—an eight-inch curve running diagonally from one side of my pubic area up to the bottom of my rib cage. With the staples in, I looked a little like Frankenstein.

From my second transplant, I added another scar, on the other side, that mirrors it exactly. Joined together, these two scars form a smiling face, with my belly button the nose and my breasts the eyes.

These and other scars form the map of where I've been and show the routes I've traveled. I can point out the various skirmishes and destinations. Here's the site of my gallbladder removal in 2005 before my second transplant. Here's the spot between my shoulders where I had emergency dialysis when I was nineteen.

I have just as many emotional scars, but they're not as visible. And these inner wounds don't engender the same sympathy.

If you battle cancer or lupus, you're called brave and courageous; if you fight against depression, addiction, or abuse you often face stigma and blame.

At a picnic not long ago I talked to a recovering alcoholic who had become sober after long years of therapy and rehabilitation. In the process of her recovery she'd lost her job, her marriage, and ties to her family. As she told me about her abandonment as a child, her mistreatment in foster families, I could see each difficult interlude flit across her face, like scenes from a movie.

But simply looking at her, an attractive woman in her mid-thirties, with a freckled face and long auburn hair, you would never have guessed. She had no large scars that were visible on the outside, but I knew she carried them within.

Her story reminded me of an incident that happened when I was a girl. I was walking with my grandmother in a wooded area when her sweater was snagged on a thorny rosebush. After she unhooked it, I pulled on the long piece of loose wool and the whole hem started to unravel.

"No, don't do that, I have to go back and fix it," she chastised me.

When we got home, she put on her glasses, sat under a bright light, and searched back until she found the source of the snag. Only then was she able to repair it.

Similarly, if a person suffers an inner trauma and tries to ignore it and move forward, she continues to unravel until she stops and returns to the source of the original pain. Until she finds where she got stuck, then fixes or heals it, she won't be able to move forward again.

Listening to the woman at the picnic, I realized that this was the kind of laborious work she had been engaged in for years.

Our lives reside in our bodies—not just our external battles but our internal ones as well. Had this woman been in a wheelchair or lost a limb, people would have acknowledged her suffering. As it was, she had struggled alone, without sympathy or support.

When I told her just that, she began to cry and reached out and took my hand.

I like to think of scars the way they do in other parts of the world, such as Africa, where they're viewed as marks of beauty. They also can signify one's status as an initiate who belongs to a particular group. That's how I felt about the woman holding my hand, crying at the picnic—that we belonged to the same association of survivors who had suffered and prevailed.

Twenty-one

IMAGINE THAT

In his book *Psycho-Cybernetics,* Maxwell Maltz wrote: "The mind cannot tell the difference between an actual experience and one vividly imagined."

That's why our hearts race when we're watching a suspense movie. Our conscious minds may know it's a fantasy, but the primitive part of our brain isn't so sure.

In my experience, what we imagine can have both positive and negative impacts on our health and well-being.

The most humiliating moment of my life is still etched in my memory. I was in kindergarten, sitting in a circle as our teacher read a story.

I had to go to the bathroom, and I wasn't the only one. But students were only allowed to leave the classroom one at a time and only after the teacher granted permission. Sometimes when she was immersed in a lesson, as she was this day, she didn't pick anyone.

I had to go so badly that I was frantic. I waved my hand and cleared my throat, but she kept her focus on the lesson.

Finally, the pressure in my bladder overcame my obedience. I simply couldn't hold it anymore.

I felt a warm wetness stream out, watching in horror as it spread in a yellow puddle around my dress, then trickled out into the middle of the floor.

"Roxanne!" The teacher finally noticed me, and bustled me out, dripping wet and humiliated. But not before the children moved away, and burst into laughter and jeers.

That day I became labeled as the girl who wet her pants. This humiliating event stuck with me for years with a miserable adhesive.

Wetting became a source of shame, the center of my life both at school and home. All through grade school, I was so terrified that this accident would happen again that I begged my mom to meet with my teachers at the beginning of each school year. I asked her to arrange special permission for me to leave the classroom to go to the bathroom every hour.

At home, I wet the bed so frequently that my mother had to constantly change the linen. Whenever I went for a sleepover at a friend's house, she sneaked a plastic sheet in my sleeping bag.

I was urged to control myself, to hold it in, to not let go. My mother even hung a chart on my wall, and gave me a gold star when I didn't wet for a week.

This normal function grew into a source of such preoccupation that before I went to sleep, I prayed to my kidneys not to disobey, as if they were renegade organs. "Please, shut down for the night, please don't let me go."

Years later, when my kidneys failed in earnest, I was left to wonder whether the impact of the wetting accident I had in front of my entire class could have played some kind of role.

By then I'd also had evidence of the positive power of imagination and visualization.

When I was growing up, my mother sent me to a private Jewish school. Besides providing me with the best education, she also wanted me to understand my heritage. My great-grandparents had been religious, but somewhere between the generations their traditions had been lost.

In the third grade, we were shown a movie about the Holocaust. There were terrible images of gaunt men and women, bodies piled on top of each other like cords of wood. The film opened a whole world of terror and cruelty that I'd never known before, tucked in my safe enclave of Pennsylvania.

When had this happened, where, and why? The teacher provided dates and showed us maps, but there was no adequate answer for the reason. A new fear took hold of me. If this had happened once, why not again?

In the following weeks, I had horrifying nightmares where I was pulled from my family and placed on a train that sped off into the night, trailing smoke. I woke up screaming and hysterical. My mom didn't know what to do with me.

"Roxanne, it was a movie. That was a long time ago."

"But it really happened! And it wasn't that long ago—you were alive then!"

I could see that she conceded the point. She considered sending me to a therapist. But instead, she used her art therapy skills and made up something that I later called "soap therapy."

One day she brought home bags of small multicolored soaps and told me to meet her in the bathroom.

Once there, she took a handful of the soaps and threw them as hard as she could against the empty bathtub. As she did this she screamed at the top of her lungs, "To hell with you, Nazis! God damn you!"

Over and over, she pummeled the soaps against the tub. Finally, she turned to me, her face scarlet, and handed me the bag of soaps. "Now you try it."

Well, this was weird. For a second I saw us as an observer might: two females in a small Pennsylvania bathroom, throwing soap at the bathtub.

"Go on," my mother urged.

Oh well, why not? Plus it was an invitation to swear, something I normally wasn't allowed. I hesitantly took a handful of soaps from the bag, threw them down into the tub, and yelled, "Damn you, Nazis! Never again!"

We kept picking up the bits of soap and throwing them until they were shattered into tiny pieces and we stood panting and spent.

At the end, my mom turned on the water and told me to watch as the tiny bits of multicolored soap swirled down the drain. She sprayed the water until the bathtub was empty and all of the soap bits gone.

Then she said: "Okay. Now it's finished. The Holocaust is over and we'll never allow it to happen again."

Part of me knew this was symbolic—soap fragments in our tub had nothing to do with what was happening in the big, wide world.

But another part of me, one I was just starting to get in touch with, felt soothed and placated by this little drama. And after that, my nightmares disappeared.

Dispelling anxiety and worry with imagery and playacting is now a well-known technique, but my mother came up with it intuitively to deal with my fear. In fact, she and I ended up presenting this technique at several imagery and art therapy conferences.

OVER THE YEARS I'VE COME to think of illness as a confluence of various influences—DNA and environment, emotions and genes—all vying for dominance. Still, I believe there are limits to how much our thoughts—or even our actions—control.

At a conference on alternative medicine, a woman said to me, "Oh, I hear you have lupus." She studied me a moment, as if she were filing me in a category. "What did you do to cause it? It's your thoughts that make you sick."

I was so annoyed by this swift assessment, as if she were blaming me for my own disease, that I turned and walked away.

I know that mental states impact the body—that even lymph and bone marrow can be affected by emotion. But I also know that illness doesn't make easy sense or fall into simple slots. There's no single reason for lupus or most other illnesses. Even lung cancer, so commonly linked with smoking, can strike a lifelong nonsmoker, like Dana Reeve, with tragic consequences. Our health can't be explained or unraveled by looking at a single strand of our being.

When I talk to my body now, I send all aspects of myself great tenderness and hope, though I may favor my kidneys, the site of my childhood distress, with a little extra attention. I treasure the gift of that little boy donor I'll never meet, but who my body so intimately knows.

Twenty-two

PENTIMENTO

I love the notion of pentimento—an alteration in a painting revealing that the artist changed his mind about the composition during the process of painting.

In a book with that title, Lillian Hellman wrote: "Old paint on canvas, as it ages, sometimes becomes transparent. When that happens it is possible, in some pictures, to see the original lines: a tree will show through a woman's dress, a child makes way for a dog, a large boat is no longer on an open sea. That is called pentimento because the painter 'repented,' changed his mind. Perhaps it would be as well to say that the old conception, replaced by a later choice, is a way of seeing and then seeing again."

Seeing again. This has happened many times in my life, when an event has shaken me, as if by the shoulders, and changed my perception, made me see something in a new and different light.

.   .   .

MY MOTHER WAS ALWAYS self-conscious about our lack of money. "I'll bet you wish we came from a wealthy family," she'd say to me. Or: "Roxanne, I'm really sorry that we don't have more."

While none of this actually mattered to me as a child, as I became older, some of her comments began to affect my own feelings of self-worth. I grew ashamed of our tiny house with its old radiators, scuffed linoleum, and ancient fixtures. I found myself coveting the big bedrooms, multiple bathrooms, and swimming pools of my friends and neighbors.

Until one day when my mother came home from work and told me a story.

At the time, she was working as a private-duty nurse, visiting ill patients who were no longer in the hospital. Her current assignment was with a woman from one of the wealthiest families in our town.

That morning, she'd been excited about her post.

"I'm going to that mansion on Main Street—you know the one, with turrets and servants' quarters. I've been dying to see what it looks like inside."

"Who's the patient?"

"Old Mrs. Minor."

When my mother returned that afternoon, I couldn't understand why she seemed so deflated and quiet.

"What was it like?" I asked her. "Did you see the third floor? I heard it has a huge attic and widow's walk."

"No, I didn't have time."

"How about the rec room—don't they have their own bowling alley?

"I didn't look—I was too busy."

"Mom, what's wrong?"

She sat down at the table and proceeded to tell me about her morning. "I walked into this splendid house—the foyer was pink marble, the curtains were velvet, but it was freezing inside, and I couldn't find anyone. I thought a family member or someone would meet me—that's how it usually is. But when I called out, there was total silence. Then I heard a moan, like from an animal. I followed the sound down this corridor lined with art and sculpture to a library where a hospital cot was set up with this fragile old woman lying on it. 'Are you the nurse?' the woman asked me.

"'Yes,' I said.

"'I'm Mrs. Minor.'

"'Are you here alone?' I asked her.

"The old woman nodded. 'My son told me he arranged for someone to come the first of the week, but they never showed up. Are you here to help me? I'm so cold.'"

My mother stopped and shook her head. "Here was this woman, with all her millions, dehydrated and freezing, alone in this fancy house with no one who cared for her. It was one of the saddest things I've ever seen, Roxanne."

I sat down and put my arm around her. I knew she was thinking the same thing that I was. Our tiny, shabby house was at least full of love, and suddenly it looked pretty spacious.

ON ANOTHER OCCASION, when I was in my mid-twenties, my sister Bonnie and I went out together to a country-music bar. Once we settled at the table, I noticed that almost everyone was dancing—except for a guy in a wheelchair, who was sitting on the sidelines, his legs hanging lifelessly. I had an inkling of how he felt, from the days when I suffered nerve damage and was in a wheelchair myself. The longer I watched, the more pity I felt for him, and the more I imagined his feelings of despair and helplessness, merging them with mine. Soon I'd worked myself up into such a fury of identification that I decided I was going to do a good deed and talk to him, maybe even offer to push his chair onto the dance floor.

Just as I was about to walk over, the sexiest girl in the bar came out of the restroom, walked over to him, and said, "Sorry to keep you waiting, honey." She gave him a long kiss and sat down in his lap. Then he wheeled his chair onto the dance floor, and they began to move together in the most seductive dance I'd ever witnessed. His wheelchair now seemed invisible. All I could see were their eyes and embrace as they moved around the floor.

A group of women at the bar began talking about the couple, who were regulars and engaged to be married. It was clear that several of the women had a crush on him. Hearing them, I felt chastened and glad I hadn't blazed out onto the floor with my so-called charity. I realized I would have been lucky to dance with this guy, not the other way around. And I would have had to take my place behind a whole group of girls who would have gladly sat on his lap, in his wheelchair, anytime.

I had believed I was sensitive to the plight of the disabled, but in fact my views had been stereotyped and patronizing. This small event made me rethink the way I viewed disabled people—and myself.

. . .

FINALLY, I have an enduring image of Bonnie lying on a stretcher in the hospital the day before my first kidney transplant, holding something on top of her covers.

I was twenty-one, a senior in college, and my kidneys had failed nearly two years before. Since then, I was self-administering dialysis five times per day everywhere I went—in airport restrooms, hotel rooms, even at television stations between interviews.

From the time I started dialysis, Bonnie had offered many times to donate a kidney to me, but I'd brushed her offer aside. I still couldn't accept that I would ever need this serious procedure. Yet in the corner of my consciousness, I registered that my sister had initiated a rigorous routine of exercise and healthy living. For nearly two years, from the time my kidneys failed, she had begun running up to seven miles a day. She'd changed her diet, lifted weights, and done everything she could to keep her body in shape.

During this period, the nerve damage in my feet and legs had made it increasingly difficult for me to walk or stand. Doctors had warned this condition might be permanent and there was a good chance I'd never be able to walk normally again.

It was not only this assessment but also another comment that finally made me accept the severity of my condition. One day at a checkup, a nurse taking my blood wrinkled her nose as she drew near to me, "Wow, you reek of urine!" she said.

I was so ill that I had been walking around, unconsciously emitting an odor as the toxins accumulated in my body. This was the last straw.

After this comment, some part in me turned a corner and faced the facts. The next day, I called Bonnie and said to her, "Are you really serious about being a donor?"

"Of course I am," she said. I realized that this is what she had been training so hard for—she'd recognized long before I had that a transplant was inevitable.

That day when she was lying on the hospital stretcher, I walked over and asked to look at what she was holding. She smiled and held it up for me to see—an X-ray of her kidney.

"Tomorrow this is going to be yours, and she pointed to the kidney on the right. Today in my body, tomorrow in your body."

The next day, she accompanied me on one of medicine's miraculous journeys—allowing her kidney to be removed from her side, washed then iced, and attached to vessels in my pelvis, where it began functioning almost immediately.

I had always known my sister was special. Sixteen years my senior, she had forever been my lighthouse, letting me toddle behind in her protective glow. But after the transplant, I saw her again.

There was something saintly in what she did for me—handing me a future, sacrificing an organ in order to provide me with renewed life.

Twenty-three

WHAT'S IN US

Shortly after college I decided I wanted to teach a class on how to start a nonprofit organization. I wanted to share the knowledge I had gleaned over the years with others who might also want to begin their own.

I talked to one of my former professors at Rutgers University and he approved the program I designed as a one-semester special offering for that autumn. The class would meet for three hours, once a week, from September through December.

I was thrilled that I was going to be a teacher and that it would be based on my experience, not dusty textbooks or tedious methodology.

I spent the summer laboriously planning the course, outlining each session and then charting topics for every hour of the class. I wrote out note cards so I knew exactly what I would say and when I would say it. Nothing was left to chance. A would follow B in a tight chain of organization. I recited these lectures in my bedroom mirror, reminding myself to look around the room and smile.

The first day, I marched into a classroom packed with a jumble of strangers all waiting to hear what I had to offer.

Nervous but confident, I positioned myself at the lectern, introduced myself, then launched into my initial lecture. I had timed it out to the minute, even leaving places for light laughter after one of my more amusing anecdotes. But as I continued speaking, I noticed that no one was laughing or even looking particularly interested. When I scanned the audience, most of the students were staring at me blankly, as if waiting for me to begin the entertainment.

The more I spoke, the more heads I saw going down, the more eyes I saw drooping. My bullet-pointed index cards were no help to me. Despite my laborious planning, within ten minutes I had lost them. One man in the back row had even begun emitting an audible snore, while a woman in the front had taken out a file and begun working on her nails.

I felt a wave of panic as my confidence plummeted. Maybe I could sneak down a fire escape and forget the whole thing. But I was stuck—and what was worse, I empathized with how they felt. I had been bored to tears through many a lecture, and the last thing I intended to do was put a crowd of people to sleep.

So I decided to go with my heart, not my well-organized mind. Rather than preach about the steps necessary to start an organization, I decided to encourage them to tell me instead. I put down my notes and clapped my hands until all heads rose again and the students focused on me.

"Okay, let's divide up into groups of four. You have five minutes to choose a cause, then five minutes to come up with a name for your organization."

Chairs scraped, people smiled and began eyeing each other. Everyone was awake now, including the dozing man in the back row. The room was suddenly abuzz with conversation.

When they finished this initial exercise, I said, "Now I want you to establish a board of directors. What types of people would you want to sit on your board? What types of fields should they specialize in? Who could help your organization grow?"

Once they came up with a board, they went on to devise a strategic plan, including mission and vision statements, goals and objectives, and deadlines.

I left the classroom for more materials, then returned and stood at the door, watching this group of people now huddled together, talking and brainstorming, awake and engaged. I couldn't believe how exhilarated I felt.

What had happened? I had simply called on them to come up with their own solutions.

This method continued to work, no matter what subject I taught in the weeks that followed. When I focused on public relations, I told the students, "Imagine you're the editor of a newspaper. What information would you need in order to write a story?"

When I wanted to teach grant writing, I asked them to pretend they were each millionaires looking to give away funds. What would they want to know about an organization before making a donation? How would they decide what deemed the organization valuable enough to earn their money?

Throughout the semester, everything I had wanted to teach the students they came up with on their own once they were provided a few guidelines, freedom, and encouragement. They took ownership of their own organizations and became passionate about their own causes. I ended up learning from them as they became energized and involved.

This experience taught me that teaching is not so much about preaching, formulas, or orderly presentations as it is challenging others to come up with their own resources and ideas. It is not hemming them in with limits and timelines, but setting them free to express what they intuitively know.

This philosophy is what underpins an innovative organization I heard about years ago that was set up in select schools. Underperforming students, who've been labeled as bullies and troublemakers, are linked with someone in the community who's elderly or disabled, and asked to show up and be of service to them.

These are children from whom nothing is expected but failure. But something happens when they are partnered with a companion, especially one who has a challenge or disability, and asked: "What would you like to do for this person?" Instead of being looked down upon, they're given respect, responsibility, and dignity, and they rise to the occasion.

One failing inner-city young man named Doug was matched with a teenager named Mary who had severe cerebral palsy. Mary couldn't eat, walk, or talk on her own and spent her life in a wheelchair. What did Mary need that Doug could provide? It turned out that he was a computer whiz and was able to devise a method, using a mouth-held pointer that Mary could use to navigate the Internet.

Mary not only was able to connect with a whole world of new correspondence, but she also bonded with Doug and counted on his weekly lessons and visits. If he didn't show up, Mary had her mother check with his principal; she savored their weekly phone calls and remembered his birthday. For his part, Doug found a place where he was valued and considered a trusted elder. He took pride in Mary's accomplishments. This experience was so crucial that it changed his future—he ended up graduating high in his class and attending a technical school where he is planning to become a teacher.

There is so much in all of us, simply waiting to emerge, but first it needs to be challenged, nurtured, and encouraged.

When an inner-city child walks into a suburban home and helps a profoundly disabled girl navigate the world, there is magic going on. Best of all, it is happening in both of them.

Twenty-four

TO BE OF USE

Eleanor Roosevelt once said: "If anyone were to ask me what I
want out of life, I would say the opportunity for doing something useful, for in no other way, I am convinced, can true happiness be attained."

I believe this sentiment applies to all of us.

When I interview applicants for jobs in my nonprofit organization, I let them know that the work will be significant and the
pay low. But so many of the applicants, especially women in
midlife, reply with a variation of Roosevelt's comment: "It's not
the money that matters to me—I want to contribute and make a
difference."

To be of use gives our days meaning and focus. And it is especially crucial for those of us who face chronic illness, who feel
physically diminished, dependent on others, stripped of our prior
identities.

We don't realize how our illness experience has also been the
most intense of educations. I tell patients to consider themselves

part of a college they never applied to but were chosen to attend by special scholarship—one that has provided them with rich reservoirs of wisdom and a deeper appreciation for life.

How can they share this? By extending a hand to others who are embarking on the same journey.

Recently I was asked to serve as the keynote speaker at the tenth anniversary of a program that does just that. Partners in Healing posts cancer survivors at a local cancer center. Whenever a new patient receives chemo or any other cancer-related diagnosis or treatment, a cancer survivor is on call at the hospital to answer questions and offer support. By their mere presence, these veterans show that survival is not only possible, but often probable. And seeing and interacting with a healing volunteer is often the best medicine.

These volunteers have experienced the wrenching moment when a doctor walks in and delivers a diagnosis; they know how it feels to have the word "cancer" suddenly affixed to their names. They know what it's like to have family and friends suddenly treat them with a new mixture of fear, avoidance, or oversolicitousness. These are all areas of special expertise that only those who have experienced illness can know.

This volunteer work provides a double blessing—while assisting others, these survivors also help themselves by gaining a sense of purpose that has emanated from their own pain.

I remember hearing a fable about a prisoner sentenced to a life of punitive labor—all day long he turned the crank of a machine that provided light for a nearby city.

It was monotonous, tedious, unending toil. But when he looked out the small window of the prison he could see illuminated lights on the horizon. Even though he was exhausted each evening, he knew he'd spent his day in a useful enterprise.

After years of work, another inmate told him: "You're a fool! You're not creating light—that's from the electric generator across town. When you turn that crank all you're doing is pushing paddles through sand in a drum. What you've been doing is completely worthless."

As it turned out, this was true—the crank was unrelated to the production of light.

When the prisoner believed he was doing something useful, he'd felt at peace; but when his illusion was burst he grew despondent, eventually sickened, and died.

THE ELDERLY ARE PERHAPS the most underutilized segment of our culture—so many are relegated to nursing homes and retirement communities, with little opportunity to share the skills and wisdom they have accumulated over a lifetime. But this is not the case in other cultures. In Okinawa, Japan, for example, elders are a central, revered part of community life, working far into old age and passing on their skills to others.

Feeling useful doesn't have to entail grand acts; even the smallest can matter.

After school, when I was a girl, I went to the home of an elderly neighbor, Mrs. Lheovis, who with her white bun and sweet face looked straight out of a fairy tale. Each afternoon she hobbled to the door on a cane to greet me. She'd lost a leg at some point in the past, and a husband in the war, but that didn't stop her from living with zest and pleasure.

She invited over neighborhood women to hand-sew quilts that were distributed to the needy; her homemade noodles dried on a rack in a back bedroom to be sold at her church bazaar. She was a skilled knitter and crocheter, and I sat beside her for hours, watching her quick hands and silver needles. Often she gave me a ball of yarn to hold as she worked away and told me when to let it out, so I felt part of the operation. She taught me to cross-stitch, cast on yarn, and purl, lessons that seemed from another century. I couldn't help comparing her to the grandmothers of some of my friends, who sat in small rooms in the local nursing homes, their hands useless and still.

Mrs. Lheovis was only supposed to be watching me until my mother returned home from work, but the small lessons she gave me meant so much to both of us. I've never forgotten the skills she imparted or the obvious pleasure she took in passing them along.

Years later, when I was driving through our old neighborhood, I pulled over and idled in front of her house. I knew she had died years before, but I still felt a throb of sadness when I saw a young couple walk out of her front door. It seemed to me that everything was exactly the same on the old cul-de-sac in East Paterson, New Jersey, except all the people I'd loved were gone.

Then I realized this wasn't true. I've knit and crocheted and tried to make the best with what I have straight through my life and illness, and whenever I do so, I'm still in the able company of Mrs. Lheovis.

To be of use—it's what all of us yearn for and deserve.

Twenty-five

THE SECRET OF HAPPINESS

The other day my husband and I were visiting a long-lost friend of mine who had recently become very wealthy. He and his wife aren't celebrities, but you wouldn't have known it from the scale of the homes we passed as we drove down their street.

"These places are like museums," I said to Leo. I couldn't imagine how single families lived in these mammoth, sprawling homes.

Inside my friend's house were marble hallways, vaulted ceilings, and multiple living rooms. Somehow all this made me nervous. Like a dog looking for the right place to sit, I kept wandering from one room to the next, trying to find a cozy corner to retreat.

As we sat having drinks in the massive dining room, I kept wondering what my Russian great-grandparents, who grew up in the pinched world of another century, would think if they walked into this room and joined us. Would they believe they'd entered a palace? That they were visiting royalty?

By the standards of human history it seemed that way even to me. We were drinking out of crystal goblets, being served wine and cheese that were once available only to the most privileged, in a neighborhood filled with swimming pools, artificial waterfalls, and luxury cars.

But more crucially, I thought my ancestors would wonder why the inhabitants didn't seem particularly happy or satisfied, given all this opulence.

For instead of appearing wildly grateful for the sheer square footage, multiple flat-screen TVs, and gorgeous vistas, my friend and his wife both seemed aggrieved and dissatisfied. The wife spent her days golfing, taking yoga classes, and playing tennis, yet she never stopped complaining—about her neighbors, her children's teachers, her husband's long hours. For his part, my friend seemed harried and anxious, pacing the vast rooms, his eye on the stock market channel.

Research suggests that once our basic needs are met, material possessions do not significantly contribute to our happiness.

Humans seem to rapidly respond to good things by taking them for granted. The more affluent we are, the more we feel we need to boost our contentment.

In fact, studies of self-reported happiness—what people tell researchers—show some surprising results, according to Edward Diener, a psychologist at the University of Illinois. As a group, older people appear more consistently satisfied with their lives than younger ones; millionaires are no more happy than those with average incomes; and the chronically ill and disabled report a slightly *higher* sense of well-being than the general population.

So what *does* bring contentment? Strong ties to friends and family as well as religious faith seem to lift the spirit, along with such boosters as practicing gratitude and performing acts of kindness.

None of these seemed evident in my friend's opulent world. But they're all present in a story I recently heard of a middle-aged Manhattan banker who was diagnosed with a serious cancer and given only a brief time to live. He quit his stressful job at an investment firm and moved to Santa Fe, near his son and family. At the same time as he established a philanthropic foundation and began divesting his fortune, he started a business based on his favorite hobby—hot-air ballooning. Each day, he transported customers into the sky and made them—and himself—happy in the process. He took up violin, reconnected with his wife, and did all the things he had planned to do in some distant retirement. While he had been expected to die after a few months, after five years, he was still surviving with joy and zest.

Rabbi Harold Kushner, best known for his book *When Bad Things Happen to Good People,* written after the death of his own son, recently spoke for our organization. Kushner has spent his life helping people find meaning and contentment despite life's suffering and disappointment. I like what Kushner has to say about happiness. He recommends that "we learn to recognize the pleasures of every day, food and work and love and friendship, as encounters with the divine, encounters that teach us not only that God is real but that we are real too."

In my case, I know I was relieved to leave my friend's splendid home and return to our own house and curl up in my favorite room. We call it the family room because it's full of items passed down from both my and Leo's families—a pair of bookcases that were a wedding gift to Leo's parents from his grandparents, a rocker that once belonged to his grandmother and that Leo himself rocked in when he was a child, walls of sepia photos—possessions that aren't worth a dime to anyone but us. I like to sit in the rocker and look at the walls, lined with memories, beloved faces from the past and present.

This room is also near the kitchen where I can smell the dinner simmering, and from a window I can view the bird feeder, busy with cardinals and blue jays feasting on sunflower seeds. These small daily pleasures are an internal wealth that no one can take away from me.

The Talmud asks: "Who is wealthy?" And it answers: "He who is content with what he has."

In the end, this is happiness: savoring our journey in the middle of living it.

Twenty-six

THE SOUND OF MUSIC

"Happy days are here again,
The skies above are clear again."

Barbra Streisand would have been surprised to learn how often I listened to her voice singing those upbeat words during the early years of my illness, when I spent more time in the hospital than at home, more time in bed than on my feet, when my future seemed a landscape of procedures, surgeries, and uncertainty.

Music has always played such a significant role during my times of illness that whenever I entered the hospital, the first thing I packed were my tapes, CDs, and headphones. I had theme songs, certain tunes that helped calm me whenever I was facing painful procedures. There was nothing I could do to change the experience except to alter my mind, and music did that.

As IVs pumped medication into my veins, I pumped my brain full of happy, upbeat music, drenching myself in sound. I listened as I faced long needles, as I was wheeled down hallways into operating suites and drifted off into unconsciousness.

During painful injections and treatments I would listen to Streisand's voice and visualize when happy, pain-free days would come again. Music didn't just distract me, it brought back the self that had been lost and fractured through illness. It filled my brain so there wasn't room for fear and dread.

Then the moment I was released, I blasted the same song in my car, in gratitude that I was finally free from the hospital.

The neurologist Oliver Sacks has written about the nearly universal responsiveness of humans to music, how many of his patients have emerged and awoken to its sound.

I didn't need proof of the great power of music to enrich and uplift. I was already aware of this from my family, who happily pushed aside their dinner plates to gather at the piano and belt out old-time favorites with gusto as I was growing up.

Even when they visited me in the hospital, they burst into song and sometimes even danced around my bed. The doctors and nurses poked their heads in, incredulous. The hospital was normally a somber place. What was going on? Did my family forget that I was lying there, hooked to IVs and monitors? Well, that was the point—they did forget it, and more important, as I listened to them break into three-part harmony, they made me briefly forget it too.

During another early hospital stay when my prognosis was uncertain, an elderly African-American cleaning woman came to my room at six each evening, an hour when the light was fading and I often felt a swoon of fear and dread.

"How're you doing, honey?" she asked as she clanked in with her mops and buckets.

While she cleaned my room, she sang gospel songs in a soft contralto; "Amazing Grace" was a daily offering. As I heard her sing "I once was lost, but now am found," I felt she was conveying to me a timeless message of hope.

For several weeks, her music was the highlight of my day. Once I was discharged, I realized I'd never even learned her name.

It was in remembrance of her that I later instituted a music-therapy program through Friends' Health Connection, where a music therapist and guest musicians go to hospitals and visit seriously ill patients at their bedsides.

Hospitals are noisy, chaotic places where people feel anxious, fearful, and disconnected. Music can help them relax and reconnect to positive thoughts from their outside lives.

In one case in early 2007, a husband and wife in their eighties were in the room when the musicians arrived. The husband was morose and had a pained look on his face as he tried to sit on the edge of the bed.

"I've always been such an active person, but now my body's turning on me," he told the musicians. He talked about his charity work and how hard it was for him to accept that he had to slow down.

The patient and his wife were both Broadway music lovers and were thrilled when the musicians offered to play "My Favorite Things" from *The Sound of Music*. At the words, "I simply remember my favorite things," the patient wept as he sang along.

Afterward, the wife said: "That's what you need to do, honey. Instead of focusing on your sickness, think of all the things you love."

By the time the musicians left, the atmosphere in the room had been lit up by the power of song.

I NEVER MET Barbra Streisand in person, but I did meet Naomi Judd, when she agreed to speak for our organization about her own battle with illness. Her song "Love Can Build a Bridge" had been another of my theme songs, one that had accompanied me through some of my most harrowing hospital experiences.

I found myself tongue-tied when I first met Judd. It wasn't so much that she was a celebrity—a disarming presence, with her blazing-red hair and porcelain skin. It was that having her voice in my head so often made me feel she was a personal friend, intimately aware of the trials and tribulations to which her music had been an unwitting accompaniment.

"You have no idea the places your music has been with me," I told her, thinking of the drab waiting rooms and the brightly lit surgeries. And I could see that I was right; she couldn't. An artist never knows where her work will have an impact.

That day, Judd, who had already struggled with single motherhood, domestic abuse, and poverty, spoke about her fight to survive the potentially fatal hepatitis C virus, a liver infection that can lead to cirrhosis, liver failure, or cancer.

At one point, her doctors had given her three years to live—a prognosis she'd refused to accept. She told our group: "The human body moves along the path of expectation. Your belief becomes your biology—what you think about, you become. . . ."

Listening to her talk made me realize that those upbeat songs had been woven into the very fabric of my existence, into a future that I was beginning to live.

Sometimes now, passing a mirror, I stop and savor the reflection of the healthy woman I've become, living the happy days that once were mere music in my ear.

Twenty-seven

CONNECTIONS

L istening to the radio the other day, I heard a woman from a town in India speaking of her country's stock market fall in relation to the United State's subprime mortgage crisis. In other words, the effect of a spate of bad loans in Des Moines and Detroit had trickled across continents to adversely affect the rupees in her distant account.

But financial markets are the least of it—whether we realize it or not, we are all bound together, starting on the most fundamental of levels.

Western science teaches us to view ourselves as private islands, separate universes of organs and bones. Spirit, mind, and body are distinct from each other, requiring specialists—ministers, psychiatrists, physicians—to treat them.

But many other cultures believe that these facets are not just interrelated—but that we are, in turn, all connected with one another.

Deepak Chopra once spoke to us about a course he held at his center, where more than one hundred and fifty people were wearing special watches that monitored heart rate and cardiovascular performance.

These heart monitors consisted of belts worn across the chest. The belt picked up a person's heart rate and transferred it to a watch—amplifying it so you can view the heart rate.

Once they were strapped up with these monitors, many people in the room suddenly began feeling dizzy. Others experienced a rapid heart rate, while still others developed uneven beats or arrhythmias.

Chopra immediately told everyone to take their monitors off and they istantly felt better. What had happened? Everyone's heartbeat was interfering with everyone else's.

This, Chopra realized, is happening all the time; this experiment only amplified it. Who we are is broadcasting itself right this moment through the beat of our hearts. The monitors only amplified the signals, creating an "interheartbeat" that people responded to in their own unique ways.

Chopra reminded us that our bodies are not just static anatomy, but flowing rivers that are constantly changing. Each time we inhale, we bring into our body over a thousand atoms—raw material from the universe. I'm breathing everything that's inside of you and vice versa. We're actually exchanging atoms all the time. As Chopra put it: "Right this moment, you have in your physical body at least a million atoms that were once in the body of Christ, or the Buddha or Michelangelo . . . "

The effect of this is far-reaching, meaning that we are not only part of each other but also the world and the environment. Chopra says: "Nature is our extended body. . . . The trees are our lungs. The rivers are circulation. The air is our breath."

This is so foreign to our Western way of thinking, where we walk around in our pods of separate consciousness, perceiving our private woes and illnesses.

But what if this were true? What if we're not distinct sites of consciousness, you and me, but only a small part of some unified whole?

Another of our past speakers, author and health educator Dr. Larry Dossey, believes in the existence of this nonlocal mind which connects us all and is spread infinitely through time and space, unconfined to an individual body.

As Dossey says: "I am not separate from my patient or a boy I see walking on the beach or an old man dying in Bombay. They are at this very moment breathing air from the same universe as I am living under the same dome of sky."

Dossey finds evidence of this consciousness, which can radiate outside a single body and impact others, in studies of distant healing and intercessory prayer.

Several studies have looked at the effects of distant prayer on illness. One involved angioplasty patients who were simultaneously prayed for by different sects around the world—Carmelite nuns in Baltimore, North Carolina Baptists, Buddhists from Nepal. These studies were double-blind, so neither the patients nor the staff was aware who was being prayed for. At the end of the study, researchers found that those who received prayer were clinically better than those who did not, reporting fewer adverse outcomes compared with those in standard therapy.

Not all later studies replicated these results, but whatever the controversy, I can vouch for prayer's efficacy on a personal level. My own family has long been involved in its own informal research.

Whenever I was going through the peaks of my illness, each member of my family prayed for my health in their own distinctive way. My mother elicited prayers from her local temple, where prayers for the ill are a regular part of the Jewish service, with synagogue members submitting names of the ailing for the rabbi to announce. She also asked far-flung members of our family to go to their windows at a certain time each evening, and send me their loving thoughts all together, from wherever they lived.

In her Catholic congregation, my sister Bonnie asked for prayers of intercession for me, a part of every mass.

My sister Wendy, an Earth Mother, concentrated on making Native American prayer ties, wrapping tobacco into pieces of cloth that she tied as she offered prayers for me. I also went with her to a sweat lodge, a dark inferno of a tepee, for a sacred purifying ceremony of renewal.

Prayer, according to Dr. Mitchell Krucoff, a professor of medicine and cardiology, "is the most ancient, widely practiced therapy on the face of the earth."

In the end, science may not be able to quantify or measure its effects. But I was grateful for all of it, for this concentration of communal, loving energy.

Perhaps more than most, I have a sense of life's deep interconnection. I walk across the room today because of the collective resources of other humans who are physically far from me. And it is not just their organs they have shared, but something more ineffable—their precious wishes of hope and love.

Twenty-eight

HEALING THE HEALER

As patients, we don't think of the burdens and trials of our physicians, but of course they have them.

In the early days of my illness I met Dr. Mehmet Oz, before he became a best-selling author or an *Oprah* regular, and he was always a great support to me, compassionate, and down to earth.

Encouraging patients to be partners in their own healing, he helped empower them by incorporating integrative methods into his surgery practice at New York City's Columbia Presbyterian Medical Center.

The first time Dr. Oz spoke for Friends' Health Connection, I surprised him by inviting a few of his former heart transplant patients to attend, including Joe Torre's brother, Frank, from Florida.

Frank and several others came up to the podium and spoke about how the transplants Dr. Oz had performed had not simply saved them, but also provided them with years of healthy life.

At the end of our event I walked up to Dr. Oz and said, "It must be extremely gratifying to have saved so many patients."

His response surprised me. "It's the ones I couldn't save that stay with me."

Before that I hadn't actually considered how much responsibility and obligation doctors carry.

Dr. Mimi Guarneri, a cardiologist, spoke to our organization about her transformation from a conventionally trained Western doctor—harried, overworked, and with potential heart issues of her own—to the founder and medical director of the Scripps Center for Integrative Medicine.

Even as an overwhelmed medical student, it had become clear to Guarneri that she wouldn't be valued for empathy or instinct, but for diagnostic speed and conciseness.

"You're not a therapist," she was reminded whenever she became distracted by a patient's life.

Her model was the cool, efficient male clinicians, who marched through rounds, godlike, dispensing brisk diagnoses. Illnesses were to be named, then cured. The complex histories of the people who were their carriers were considered incidental.

When faced with a broken arm or heart, she was urged to use splints and stents, mechanical devices to quickly fix them. As Lewis Thomas wrote, medicine had become no longer "the laying on of hands . . . but more like reading signals from machines."

Because Guarneri did not want to be viewed as weak, she tried to keep her feelings of curiosity and empathy at bay.

As Dr. Larry Dossey writes: "In medical school, women often try to out-macho the men, in order to simply cope with the pressures of school. A lot of the feminine intuitive instincts are overwhelmed by the experience of becoming a doctor."

Luckily, Guarneri had early influences that were as potent as her medical training.

She came from a line of doctors who followed the old traditions, including an uncle, a GP in Long Island, who diagnosed without sophisticated equipment, but by following his instincts, listening to his patients, and utilizing his years of expertise.

Despite her medical training, these influences continued to perk away in her. They resurfaced in the middle of a career in which she had increasingly begun to feel like a plumber—spending her days unblocking the arteries of patients who left the hospital without changing their lives, often returning with new blockages a few years later.

In her book *The Heart Speaks,* she writes: "I spent my days propping open their arteries with metal sleeves called stents without considering why they had closed in the first place."

In the meantime, Guarneri was so overworked that she had to face her own overstressed body and family history of cardiac disease. When Dr. Dean Ornish arrived at Scripps to initiate a program to reverse coronary disease with diet, exercise, meditation, and support, she joined in. She was so impressed with the results on her own health and that of her patients, she gradually incorporated them into her practice.

She also began to honor the old-fashioned virtues that physicians were once so valued for—taking time beyond the typical seven-minute office visit to develop rapport and compassionate interactions with patients.

Like Drs. Oz and Guarneri, Dr. David Laskow is both a renowned physician and a compassionate and caring healer, the director of kidney and pancreas transplant surgery at Robert Wood Johnson University Hospital in New Brunswick, New Jersey.

I met with him before my second transplant surgery, during those frightening days when it was clear that my first kidney was failing, that I needed to go back on dialysis again and would require another transplant.

I already had grown accustomed to the nerve-wracking monthly bloodwork that monitored my kidney function. These tests felt like a constant audition. How would I fare this time? In spite of anything I might do in terms of healthy living, these numbers could change at any moment and blast a hole into my best-laid plans. I could be feeling perfectly well, but the numbers on a sheet of lab work could indicate otherwise.

One afternoon, I returned to the doctor's office for my results following a visit to Panera Bread. This was where I always went to give myself a treat after my bloodwork while I waited for my verdict. I ordered my favorite bagel—Asiago cheese toasted with butter—and savored the crunch and warmth with a cup of coffee.

Time after time, I'd returned from my bagel break with dread in the pit of my stomach only to be told that my bloodwork numbers were still fine. I would exit the clinic feeling the thrill of reprieve and a renewed sense of luck and life.

Then, all at once, everything changed; the level of creatinine (a normally occurring byproduct of the breakdown of phosphate in muscles) in my bloodstream was too high and that meant my kidney was in trouble. It was happening all over again. It was at this vulnerable time that I met Dr. David Laskow, who performed the surgery to reattach the port I would need to self-administer dialysis again while I awaited a new kidney.

I was devastated. There had been no way to know for certain how long my first transplant would last, but I had hoped it would keep me healthy for many more years.

Dr. Laskow sat down with me and said, "I know how you feel—but I'm telling you, I have no worries about your outcome."

He looked in my eyes as he spoke; he took my hand.

These small gestures were of immense comfort.

I held on to his certainty like a talisman or lucky charm for all those frightening months waiting for another organ. I believed in him, and he was right.

As a transplant surgeon, Laskow had presided over thousands of miracles and was well-known for saving lives.

When asked once why he had chosen the field of transplantation, he replied: "Not only does it require you to be highly skilled, but it is cutting edge, and this appealed to me intellectually as well."

But fate had another reason.

On a Saturday morning in 2005, Laskow, who had just turned fifty, was alone at home when he started experiencing chest pain and dizziness.

He managed to call a neighbor before he lost consciousness. When he awoke two weeks later in the hospital, he had been intubated and was suffering from a serious infection.

He was informed that he'd not only had a heart attack, but also suffered renal, respiratory, and liver failure. He had been put on a mechanical heart, and doctors were worried about a stroke.

His family put out the word that the well-known transplant surgeon now needed a heart transplant of his own.

He was placed on the waiting list for a transplant with the New Jersey Organ and Tissue Sharing Network.

When no appropriate donors were located in New Jersey, and his condition deteriorated, the search was broadened. Finally, a match was found, the heart of a fifty-one-year-old woman from Delaware who'd spent her own life helping the handicapped.

In the hospital after his transplant, Laskow's struggles continued: he became infected with a drug-resistant bacteria and was unable to breathe on his own. But by January 2006—fifty pounds lighter—he finally regained liver and kidney function and was released.

In November 2007, I hosted a dinner for my organization during which I honored Dr. Laskow's service. Although he had always regarded me with compassion and respect, I felt a new bond between us as he walked up on the stage and gave me a hug.

Most physicians specialize in a particular illness or procedure, but few have experienced firsthand the personal challenges and realities that their patients face.

Time is always ticking underneath our lives, but after a transplant, the tick is audible. The provisional state of your health is always there in the forefront of your mind.

Dr. Laskow knew both sides now. We were both in the same fraternity—the transplant club, I call it.

Others might have retired or rested on their laurels after such an ordeal, but not Dr. Laskow. As I write this, he's back at Robert Wood Johnson University Hospital at his old post at the operating table, working to save more lives, as his was saved.

Twenty-nine

SIGNS

I consider myself the mutt in my family in more ways than one—
a mix of everyone before me—especially my mother and two
sisters.

Certainly, in terms of religion, I've taken a little from each of
their columns. When I was a girl, my mother used to fondly describe a temple my grandparents and relatives attended in Allentown, Pennsylvania, when she was little. It was a very old and
beloved Orthodox synagogue, where the women sat in an upper
area, separated from the men. From her upstairs perch, my mother
watched the men in her family praying together, standing and bow-
ing. At some point in the service, they turned and winked at her. I
loved to imagine this scene as a child—my relatives involved in
traditions and customs that seemed from another world.

Fast-forward twenty years, when after my mother's death I set
up offices in a historic section of New Brunswick, New Jersey.
One day, walking to my office, I passed a small, beautiful temple
called Poile Zedek and felt compelled to walk in. It was a little
jewel box, full of stained glass and a warm, welcoming feeling. As

I stepped inside, I felt I was standing in the site of my mother's memories. Later I discovered that the temple was erected in 1923, around the time of my mother's stories, and that the original congregants had been Russian and Polish. I didn't know anyone there, but I felt immediately at home.

On the next high holy day, I began a tradition of my own: I put on a skirt and my husband accompanied me to services in the little temple. As a Catholic, Leo didn't know a word of Hebrew, but that didn't stop him from donning a yarmulke, and sitting apart from me in the special men's section. From my perch, I watched him follow the lead of the other men, standing and sitting on cue, eventually turning around and giving me a sheepish wave and smile. I felt reconnected to my past as we reenacted the scene my mother had once so lovingly described.

I also love the ceremony and majesty that are part of my sister Bonnie's Catholicism.

One Christmas Eve, when I was still single and feeling lonely, I lay in bed listening to the radio. It was nine o'clock at night when I heard the announcement: "Coming up at midnight we'll broadcast mass live from St. Patrick's Cathedral."

I'd gone to St. Patrick's in the past when I felt dispirited. I loved how all that grandeur was free and available to anyone.

After I heard the announcement, it was suddenly clear to me where I needed to be that night. I got out of bed and threw on my clothes. Even though I lived an hour away from Manhattan and it was pitch dark and freezing, I drove myself to the cathedral.

When I arrived, I walked up the steps to find myself in a long line of congregants, waiting to get in.

A woman in front of me said, "You can't attend unless you have tickets, and it was sold out months ago."

At this news, other people walked away, discouraged, but I wasn't about to give up. But how would I ever get in? I frantically tried to come up with a plan as people milled past me, bustling into the gorgeous vaulted interior that I could glimpse even from the street.

When I couldn't figure out a way to gain entrance and began crying, a guard walked over and asked, "Are you okay?"

"I didn't realize I needed a ticket. I just drove all the way from New Jersey."

I must have looked desperate—a waif alone in the night. When no one was looking, the guard sneaked me in through a door on the side.

As the organ began playing, I walked down the candlelit aisle under those immense ceilings, through the scent of wafting incense.

I was right: this was where I needed to be. I felt such solace and gratitude that Christmas Eve to worship in such a sacred place.

And then there was my sister Wendy and her Native American beliefs. When I was a girl, she took me most afternoons to a pond at a nearby park to feed the ducks. One day we were sitting on a rock when a spider crawled by. When I screamed and stepped on it, she became furious. "How could you kill an innocent spider! We're outdoors in *its* home, not the other way around."

She went on to tell me how spiders were creatures of power in the Native American tradition and that there were many stories and legends about spiders and webs.

Wendy had already given me a dream catcher, a handmade hoop of willow in the shape of a spiderweb, to hang above my bed, as a charm against bad dreams.

And she also utilized other Native American beliefs in an attempt to help with my illness. One of her favorites was smudge sticks—herbs that are tightly bound together and wrapped with string. When lit, the smoke is waved around people and homes to cleanse the surrounding energy.

Before my first transplant, Wendy arrived at the hospital with a smudge stick in her satchel and asked my mother and sister Bonnie to accompany her to the parking lot for a purifying ceremony.

I stood at the window and watched as she lit the stick and started waving it around, then held it aloft as the three of them stood together and closed their eyes as if they were praying.

This was all to the perplexity of others in the parking lot, who rushed by them as if they were crazy.

Except for one man, a little scruffy, who I saw approach them from the street.

I watched as he walked up to Wendy and said something, which she reacted to with obvious outrage.

Later when she stomped back into my room, surrounded by a fragrant cloud of incense, she was incensed.

"What's the matter?"

"The nerve! He thought we were burning marijuana and asked me to sell him some!"

Although I didn't always understand some of the techniques my sister used when I was young, many of her beliefs seeped into me nonetheless. Because of her, I am more respectful of nature. And there is this: I've never stepped on a spider again.

I find all these belief systems beautiful and interesting and have taken a bit from each of them into my own concept of religion and God.

But what about the afterlife, the preoccupation of most religions? I'm never exactly sure what I believe.

Most Christians have faith that there is some kind of heaven, in which believers enjoy the presence of God and freedom from suffering and sin.

Catholics also believe in purgatory, a temporary place of punishment for Christians who have died with unconfessed sins.

In the Jewish religion, focus is more on earthly life, and the fulfillment of duties to God and one's fellow man. Whether the spirit endures after death isn't considered as crucial.

And then there are Eastern religions and their various beliefs about the continuation of the spirit. When I first heard Deepak Chopra speak about reincarnation, I found myself yearning to join in his belief that I might return one day in another form.

I remember being somewhat skeptical when a friend of mine who had lost a beloved brother at a young age went to a psychic. Her brother had died without warning, and in her disbelief and grief, my friend hoped for some sign from him.

The psychic, who lived in a suburban house, was an unassuming older women. She sat my friend at the dining room table, asked for an item from the loved one, and then closed her eyes and fell into what seemed like a trance.

"This is a man, is that right?"

"Yes," my friend said.

"Is it your father?"

"No."

"Your brother?"

"Yes."

The psychic was silent for a moment. "Well, I have a message," she said. "Your brother said that he loves the color of your new car."

My friend broke into tears at this statement—the week before she'd bought a red Jeep, her brother's favorite color—and began weeping again when she told me.

I was amazed at how comforted she was by this little shard of information. And a part of me also couldn't help wondering this: of all the information her brother could have communicated from the other side, why wasn't it something more significant than the color of a car? Still, I was sobered by the effect this communication had on my friend and gratified by her obvious relief.

I had a similar reaction not long after, when a college friend lost her mother after a long illness. My friend was an only child, and particularly close to her mother and her grief was terrible.

One afternoon, not long after the wake, she came to see me, her face ashen.

"What's wrong?"

"The strangest thing just happened."

She and her mother had a private communication that involved yellow roses. They gave them to each other for birthdays and other special events. It was something no one else knew.

That morning as she opened her apartment door to go to work, there was a bouquet of yellow roses sitting outside on her front stoop, without a card or florist name.

"It was a message from her, it had to be," she told me.

My practical mind was searching for other explanations—

surely other family members knew about this or a friend had simply left a bouquet not knowing its significance. There were only a few florists who delivered in her area; she could call them and ask if they had delivered the bouquet and who had sent it.

But as I watched my friend's face, I knew I would voice none of these ideas; she didn't really want to hear them.

She may have been upset by this gift, but a part of her was comforted by it. It was a precious link to her. In the days that followed, it seemed that her grief was lessened.

But I didn't truly understand the desire for such a sign until something similar happened to me.

When my mother died, shortly before my twenty-fifth birthday, we'd planned to go to a Broadway show and celebrate at dinner. But there I was on my birthday, devastated.

The hardest thing about death is that it marks the end of hope. Even though she'd fought hard to hide it, my mother had been ill for many years and had almost died a number of times from severe asthma. But she always pulled through—there was always a filament of hope to hold on to—she was always still there, the breath in her chest, the white square of light in her eye.

Now, suddenly, it was really over. Her body lay lifeless, a shell, in a funeral home nearby. That I was never going to hear her voice at the end of the phone or see her alive again seemed both impossible and unbearable, and left me in a paroxysm of grief.

My sister Bonnie eventually found me, buried under the covers, weeping. "Roxanne, you have to pull yourself together," my sister said. "Come on, get up. It's your birthday."

She was grieving too, I realized, and so I got up and took a shower and we had dinner together.

But after she left, I realized I still had to get through the rest of this birthday evening. The only thing I could think to do was the most prosaic of tasks—the laundry.

I went down to the laundry room in the basement and came upon a stack of boxes. I knew my mother had been cleaning out her storage room and had given me some boxes to keep, but I hadn't paid much attention or even looked inside of them. When I took the lid off one of the boxes, there was a huge pile of what looked to be hundreds of cassette tapes. My mother had been a great chronicler, filming and taping us as children growing up, but these had been stored in her typical jumbled fashion, and I had no idea what they were.

I randomly picked up one from the top and took it upstairs. I saw that it was dusty and unlabeled. So I wiped it off, placed it in the cassette player, and pressed Play.

Out came a younger version of the voices of my mother and me:

"Mommy, do you want to sing our song?" I asked.

"Sure, let's do it."

We began to sing "Do You Love Me?" from *Fiddler on the Roof* with our own distinctive lyrics:

"Do you love me?"

"Do I love you? For all the years I've washed your clothes. Cooked your meals, cleaned your room. If that's not love, what is?"

After a few more verses, my mother ended: "Happy birthday, honey."

I sat there in the dark, her words still hanging in the air. We'd recorded this tape exactly fifteen years earlier on my tenth birthday. That I'd discovered it by chance on this particular dark evening made my skepticism float out the door.

I now accept that there's a higher power that sends us signs that our loved ones are never lost.

When I hear my mother's laugh emerge from my throat or see my profile in the mirror and glimpse my grandmother, I know this to be true on a personal level. We're all walking encyclopedias of those who came before us. Still alive, after all.

Afterword

I logged on to the website for CBS News recently to find an article that amazed me. The headline read: "Medicine's Cutting Edge: Re-Growing Organs."

The first paragraph read:

Imagine re-growing a severed fingertip, or creating an organ in the lab that can be transplanted into a patient without risk of rejection. It sounds like science fiction, but it's not. It's the burgeoning field of regenerative medicine, in which scientists are learning to harness the body's own power to regenerate itself, with astonishing results.

The article went on to describe how a man sliced off the tip of his finger in the propeller of a hobby-shop airplane. His brother, a medical research scientist, sent him a special powder and told him to sprinkle it on the wound.

To his astonishment, his entire fingertip grew back. According to Dr. Stephen Badylak of the University of Pittsburgh's McGowan

Institute of Regenerative Medicine, the powder, a mixture of protein and connective tissue, told the body to begin the process of tissue regrowth.

Badylak is one of many scientists who are now convinced that all tissue in the body contains cells that are capable of regeneration, if scientists can only locate enough of them and urge or "direct" them to grow.

Some scientists even believe that it's only a matter of time before it's possible to grow a human heart.

This story amazed me and filled with me with hope. While I waited with trepidation for my own transplant—and watched others do the same—I sometimes imagined a fantasy future, where organs could be grown or regenerated from the cells of our bodies. Now I had lived long enough to see that this can become a reality.

And I couldn't help imagining how the people I've loved and lost would react to such stunning developments—my mother and Christopher Reeve, Ruby and my friend Laura.

These advances reinforce my belief that there are always new transformations on the horizon, right beside the unexpected blessings of everyday life—regenerative research along with a hand clasped at a picnic, a gospel song hummed in a hospital, a balloon of hope and human connection rising into the cloudless sky.

Selected Bibliography

Alda, Alan. *Things I Overheard While Talking to Myself.* New York: Random House, 2007.

Chopra, Deepak. *The Book of Secrets: Unlocking the Hidden Dimensions of Your Life.* New York: Harmony, 2004.

Dossey, Larry. *Reinventing Medicine: Beyond Mind-Body to a New Era of Healing.* New York: HarperOne, 2000.

Groopman, Jerome. *The Anatomy of Hope: How People Prevail in the Face of Illness.* New York: Random House, 2005.

Guarneri, Mimi. *The Heart Speaks.* New York: Simon and Schuster, 2005.

Hellman, Lillian. *Pentimento.* Boston: Back Bay, 2000.

Judd, Naomi. *Naomi's Breakthrough Guide: 20 Choices to Transform Your Life.* New York: Simon and Schuster, 2004.

Kirschner, Ann. *Sala's Gift: My Mother's Holocaust Story.* New York: Simon and Schuster, 2006.

Kushner, Harold. *When All You've Ever Wanted Isn't Enough: The Search for a Life That Matters.* New York: Fireside, 2002.

————. *When Bad Things Happen to Good People.* New York: Anchor, 2004.

Lauber, Lynn. *Listen to Me: Writing Life into Meaning.* New York: W. W. Norton, 2005.

Maltz, Maxwell. *Psycho-Cybernetics: A New Way to Get More Living Out of Life.* New York: Pocket, 1989.

Meili, Trisha. *I Am the Central Park Jogger: A Story of Hope and Possibility.* New York: Scribner, 2004.

Neufeld, Martin. *Hugging Life: A Practical Guide to Artful Hugging.* Montreal: Hugging Life, 2007.

Oz, Mehmet. *Healing from the Heart: A Leading Surgeon Combines Eastern and Western Traditions to Create the Medicine of the Future.* New York: Plume, 1999.

Pennebaker, James. *Opening Up: The Healing Power of Expressing Emotions.* New York: The Guilford Press, 1997.

Reeve, Christopher. *Still Me.* New York: Random House, 1998.

————. *Nothing Is Impossible: Reflections on a New Life.* New York: Ballantine, 2004.

Rollins, Betty. *Here's the Bright Side: Of Failure, Fear, Cancer, Divorce, and Other Bum Raps*. New York: Random House, 2007.

Sacks, Oliver. *An Anthropologist on Mars: Seven Paradoxical Tales*. New York: Vintage, 1996.

———. *Musicophilia: Tales of Music and the Brain*. New York: Alfred A. Knopf, 2007.

Schneider, Pat. *Writing Alone and With Others*. New York: Oxford University Press, 2003.

Siegel, Bernie. *Love, Medicine & Miracles: Lessons Learned about Self-Healing from a Surgeon's Experience with Exceptional Patients*. New York: Harper, 1990.

Resource Directory

The following is a list of services available throughout the country for people living with illness or disability, as well as their caregivers. This list is by no means exhaustive, and you will need to research each organization before getting involved to ensure accuracy of any information provided and to be sure they meet your needs.

ADVOCACY FOR PATIENTS

Patient Advocate Foundation
700 Thimble Shoals Boulevard
Suite 200
Newport News, VA 23606
800-532-5274
http://patientadvocate.org

The Patient Advocate Foundation is a national nonprofit organization that seeks to safeguard patients through effective mediation, assuring access to care, maintenance of employment, and preservation of financial stability relative to their diagnosis of life-threatening or debilitating diseases.

ASSISTANCE WITH CHORES, RIDES

Faith in Action
http://www.faithinaction.org

Click "Find a program" on the home page for a searchable list of offices categorized by state.

Faith in Action is an interfaith, volunteer, caregiving initiative. Local programs bring together volunteers from many faiths to work together to care for their neighbors who have long-term health needs. Volunteers help those in need by providing nonmedical assistance with tasks such as picking up groceries, running errands, providing rides to doctor appointments, offering friendly visits, and providing help paying bills.

CAREGIVING

Family Caregiver Alliance
180 Montgomery Street
Suite 1100
San Francisco, CA 94104
800-445-8106 or 415-434-3388
http://www.caregiver.org

Founded in 1977, Family Caregiver Alliance was the first community-based nonprofit organization in the country to address the needs of families and friends, providing long-term care at home. FCA now offers programs at national, state, and local levels to support and sustain caregivers.

Lotsa Helping Hands

http://www.lotsahelpinghands.com

Lotsa Helping Hands helps communities of caregivers stay organized with their tasks so they can better help chronically ill patients whom they love. The website offers an easy-to-use, private group calendar, specifically designed for organizing helpers. Friends and loved ones can pitch in with meals delivery, rides, and other tasks necessary for life to run smoothly during times of medical crisis, end-of-life caring, or family caregiver exhaustion. It's also a place to keep these "circles of community" informed with status updates, photo galleries, message boards, and more.

Strength for Caring

http://www.strengthforcaring.com

Strength for Caring is an online resource and community for family caregivers to help them take care of their loved ones and themselves. Strength for Caring is part of the Caregiver Initiative, created by Johnson & Johnson. Strength for Caring works with caregiving and health-care organizations across the country.

DATING

Dating4Disabled.com
201-984-5912
http://dating4disabled.com

Dating4Disabled.com is an online community that offers the opportunity for people with disabilities to share, connect, and just be heard. Make friends, find romance, and discuss resources with people from all over the world. Dating4disabled.com welcomes disabled and able-bodied members on condition that they want to meet people with disabilities and are committed to respecting all members.

EMPLOYMENT FOR PEOPLE WITH DISABILITIES

ABILITYJobs
ABILITY Mail Center
P.O. Box 10878
Costa Mesa, CA 92627
http://abilityjobs.com

By providing a dedicated system for finding employment, the goal of ABILITYJobs is to enable people with disabilities to enhance their professional lives. Employers who post job opportunities not only exhibit an open-door policy, but also demonstrate their responsiveness to affirmative action by genuinely recruiting qualified persons with disabilities.

Expressive therapies

American Dance Therapy Association (ADTA)
10632 Little Patuxent Parkway
Suite 108
Columbia, MD 21044
410-997-4040
http://www.adta.org

Founded in 1966, the American Dance Therapy Association works to establish and maintain high standards of professional education and competence in the field of dance/movement therapy.

American Music Therapy Association, Inc.
8455 Colesville Road
Suite 1000
Silver Spring, MD 20910
301-589-3300
http://www.musictherapy.org

The mission of the American Music Therapy Association is to advance public awareness of the benefits of music therapy and increase access to quality music therapy services.

The Foundation for Hospital Art
120 Stonemist Court
Roswell, GA 30076
770-645-1717
http://www.hospitalart.org

The purpose of the Foundation for Hospital Art is to give comfort and hope to those who suffer in hospitals by providing artwork at no cost to hospitals.

The National Association of Poetry Therapy

Center for Education, Training & Holistic Approaches, Inc.

777 E. Atlantic Avenue #243

Delray Beach, FL 33483

866-844-6278

http://www.poetrytherapy.org

Since 1981, NAPT members have forged a community of healers and lovers of words and language.

National Coalition of Creative Arts Therapies Associations

c/o AMTA

8455 Colesville Road

Suite 1000

Silver Spring, MD 20910

http://www.nccata.org

The National Coalition of Creative Arts Therapies Associations is an alliance of professional associations dedicated to the advancement of the arts as therapeutic modalities. NCCATA represents more than fifteen thousand individual members of six creative arts therapies associations nationwide.

Society for the Arts in Healthcare

2437 15th Street NW

Washington, DC 20009

202-299-9770

http://www.thesah.org

The Society for the Arts in Healthcare (SAH) is a nonprofit 501(c)(3) organization dedicated to promoting the incorporation of the arts as an integral component of health care.

Spontaneous Drawings

http://www.ecap-online.org/artwork.htm

Spontaneous Drawings Creative Expression is a service of Exceptional Cancer Patients (ECap), a program for cancer patients started by the renowned and much loved Dr. Bernie Siegel. You can mail Dr. Siegel your personal drawings and he will take time to review them and then e-mail you his interpretations. The goal is to help you discover the insights that can aid in your healing process. A nominal fee may apply.

Very Special Arts

818 Connecticut Avenue NW

Suite 600

Washington, DC 20006

800-933-8721

202-628-2800 (voice)

202-737-0645 (TDD)

http://www.vsarts.org

VSA is an international, nonprofit organization founded in 1974 by Ambassador Jean Kennedy Smith to create a society where all people with disabilities learn through, participate in, and enjoy the arts.

FASHION AND ACCESSORIES ESPECIALLY FOR PEOPLE WITH CHRONIC ILLNESS

MedTees.com
http://www.MedTees.com
This site sells humorous and thoughtful T-shirts about living with chronic illness.

Chronique Couture
Fort Worth, Texas
817-361-1657
http://chroniquecouture.com

This is an online boutique that sells fashionable and sassy accessories and products specially designed for those living with chronic illness.

Sun Precautions
800-882-7860 or 425-303-8585
http://www.sunprecautions.com

Sun Precautions sells sun-protective fashion for sun-sensitive and sun-sensible people.

FIND OR START A SUPPORT GROUP

American Self-Help Clearinghouse
973-989-1122
http://www.selfhelpgroups.org

The Self-Help Sourcebook Online is a keyword-searchable database that includes information on more than twelve hundred national, international, model and online self-help support groups, ideas for starting groups, local self-help group clearinghouses, and help if you want to develop any needed new national or international groups.

Information for starting a group of your own
Start your own support group
http://www.mentalhelp.net/selfhelp

You will see where it says "Starting a new mutual-aid support group." Underneath this header, you can click on either where it says "In your community," which provides information about starting a live support group in your community, or "How to Develop an Online Support Group or Web Site," which is a wonderful resource for starting a support group online. Also, on the right side of this page is a searchable list of health-related nonprofit organizations.

Funding medications

NeedyMeds.com

http://www.Needymeds.com

NeedyMeds is a nonprofit 501(c)(3) organization with the mission of helping people who cannot afford medicine or health-care costs.

Humor and happiness

Loretta LaRoche

http://www.LorettaLaRoche.com

Loretta LaRoche is an international stress management and humor consultant whose wit and irreverent humor have, for more than thirty years, raised the humor potential in all of us. She is on the Mass General advisory council for anxiety and depression and was recently awarded the National Humor Treasure Award. Organizations worldwide use Loretta's prescription for laughter to manage stress in the workplace and improve morale. Loretta's website includes "Kick of the Month" and "Loretta's community."

Tal Ben-Shahar

http://www.talbenshahar.com

Tal Ben-Shahar teaches the largest, most popular course at Harvard on Positive Psychology and the third-largest on Psychology of Leadership with a total of more than fourteen hundred students. His website includes happiness tips and articles about positive psychology.

The UCLA Norman Cousins Center for
Psychoneuroimmunology

http://www.cousinspni.org

The UCLA Cousins Center brings together research expertise in the behavioral sciences, neuroscience, and immunology to understand the interplay of psychological and biological factors in disease and how the resiliency of the human body can be aided by positive behaviors, attitudes, and emotions.

KIDNEY

National Kidney Foundation

30 East 33rd Street
New York, NY 10016
800-622-9010 or 212-889-2210
http://www.kidney.org

The National Kidney Foundation seeks to prevent kidney and urinary tract diseases, improve the health and well-being of individuals and families affected by these diseases, and increase the availability of all organs for transplantation. Its website includes a state-by-state searchable list of chapters.

LUPUS

Alliance for Lupus Research
28 West 44th Street
Suite 501
New York, NY 10036
800-867-1743 or 212-218-2840
http://www.lupusresearch.org

The Alliance for Lupus Research (ALR) is a national voluntary health organization based in New York City that was founded in 1999 and is chaired by Robert Wood Johnson IV, a member of the founding family of Johnson & Johnson. Its mission is to find better treatments and ultimately prevent and cure lupus.

Lupus Foundation of America
2000 L Street NW
Suite 710
Washington, DC 20036
202-349-1155
http://www.lupus.org

The Lupus Foundation of America is the nation's foremost national nonprofit voluntary health organization dedicated to finding the causes of, and cure for, lupus and providing support and services to all people affected by lupus. The website includes a state-by-state searchable directory of chapters.

PAIN MANAGEMENT

American Chronic Pain Association
P.O. Box 850
Rocklin, CA 95677
800-533-3231
http://www.theacpa.org

The mission of the ACPA is to raise awareness about issues of living with chronic pain among members of the health-care community, policy makers, and the public at large.

American Pain Society
4700 West Lake Avenue
Glenview, IL 60025
847-375-4715
http://www.ampainsoc.org

The American Pain Society is a multidisciplinary community that brings together a diverse group of scientists, clinicians, and other professionals to increase the knowledge of pain and transform public policy and clinical practice to reduce pain-related suffering.

RARE DISORDERS

National Organization for Rare Disorders
55 Kenosia Avenue

P.O. Box 1968

Danbury, CT 06813-1968

800-999-NORD or 203-744-0100

TDD: (203) 797-9590

http://www.rarediseases.org

The National Organization for Rare Disorders (NORD) is a unique nonprofit federation of voluntary health organizations dedicated to helping people with rare "orphan" diseases and assisting the organizations that serve them. NORD is committed to the identification, treatment, and cure of rare disorders through programs of education, advocacy, research, and service.

SUPPORT AND INSPIRATION

ButYouDontLookSick.com
http://www.butyoudontlooksick.com

ButYouDontLookSick.com is an online magazine about living life to the fullest with any disability, invisible disease, or chronic pain. There is a collection of articles, stories, and book and product reviews, with health resources and an active message board for the disabled, or those living with chronic pain or illness.

Chronic Babe

3712 North Broadway #628

Chicago, IL 60613

773-935-9246

http://www.chronicbabe.com

The mission of Chronic Babe is to help young women with chronic illness be their best . . . to be babes! They believe that empowerment can be the strongest medicine, that women who feel in control of their lives, despite their health issues, can achieve anything they put their minds to.

Daily Good's Quote of the Day

http://www.dailygood.org

Daily Good is a free daily e-mail service that delivers a little bit of inspiring goodness to 75,375 people. It is there simply to spread the good.

Friends' Health Connection

P.O. Box 114

New Brunswick, NJ 08903

800-483-7436

http://www.friendshealthconnection.org

Friends' Health Connection is a nonprofit 501(c)(3) organization that offers an unprecedented array of educational programs that encompass the well-being of mind, body, and spirit and include a complete continuum of health, wellness, motivation, and lifestyle topics. In addition, we are proud to offer a worldwide network where individuals with health challenges connect with one another for mutual support. Caregivers are welcome as well.

Hay House Radio

http://www.hayhouseradio.com

Free radio for your soul is right on your computer. This website's live, twenty-four-hour programming features some of the most notable names in health, wellness, and motivation.

TRANSPLANT

The American Organ Transplant Association

21175 Tomball Parkway #194
Houston, TX 77070
713-344-2402
http://www.aotaonline.org

The mission of the AOTA is to help transplant patients lead happy, productive lives by helping them obtain and sustain transplantation.

Since 1986, the American Organ Transplant Association (AOTA) has been helping patients with free transportation to and from their transplant center, many times hundreds of miles away. AOTA also provides transplant patients and their loved ones with resources regarding transplantation.

Transplant Recipients International Organization
2100 M Street NW #170-353
Washington, DC 20037-1233
800-TRIO-386 or 202-293-0980
http://www.trioweb.org

TRIO is an independent, not-for-profit, international organization committed to improving the quality of life of transplant candidates, recipients, their families, and the families of organ and tissue donors.

United Network of Organ Sharing
P.O. Box 2484
Richmond, VA 23218
804-782-4800
http://unos.org

The United Network for Organ Sharing (UNOS) is a nonprofit scientific and educational organization that administers the nation's only Organ Procurement and Transplantation Network, established by the U.S. Congress in 1984.

Volunteering

VolunteerMatch
717 California Street
Second Floor
San Francisco, CA 94108
415-241-6868
http://www.volunteermatch.org

VolunteerMatch is a leader in the nonprofit world dedicated to helping everyone find a great place to volunteer. The organization offers a variety of online services to support a community of nonprofit, volunteer, and business leaders committed to civic engagement.

Wish-granting

Dream Foundation
1528 Chapala Street
Suite 304
Santa Barbara, CA 93101
805-564-2131
http://www.dreamfoundation.org

Dream Foundation is the first and largest national wish-granting organization for adults with life-limiting illness. The mission of Dream Foundation is to enhance the quality of life for individuals and their families during the end of life's journey. Dream Foundation helps adults find peace and closure with the realization of a final wish.

Make-A-Wish Foundation® of America
3550 North Central Avenue
Suite 300
Phoenix, AZ 85012-2127
800-722-9474
http://www.wish.org

Make-A-Wish grants the wishes of children with life-threatening medical conditions to enrich the human experience with hope, strength, and joy.

Index

Index